# OVERWORKED, OVERWHELMED & UNDERPAID

**Other Books by Louis Barajas**

*The Latino Journey to Financial Greatness*
*Small Business, Big Life*

# OVERWORKED, OVERWHELMED & UNDERPAID

*Simple Steps to Go from Stress to Success*

# LOUIS BARAJAS

THOMAS NELSON

*Since 1798*

NASHVILLE   DALLAS   MEXICO CITY   RIO DE JANEIRO   BEIJING

Published in Nashville, Tennessee, by Thomas Nelson. Thomas Nelson is a registered trademark of Thomas Nelson, Inc.

Editorial Staff: Joel Miller, acquisitions editor; Thom Chittom, managing editor
Page Design: Lori Lynch

Thomas Nelson, Inc., titles may be purchased in bulk for educational, business, fund-raising, or sales promotional use. For information, please e-mail SpecialMarkets@ThomasNelson.com.

The stories in this book are drawn from the experiences of Mr. Barajas's clients. Some are composites of several different individuals. In all cases, names and identifying information have been changed.

**Library of Congress Cataloging-in-Publication Data**

Barajas, Louis, 1961–
  Overworked, overwhelmed, and underpaid : simple steps to go from stress to success / by Louis Barajas.
    p. cm.
  Includes bibliographical references.
  1. Job satisfaction. 2. Quality of work life. 3. Work and family. I. Title.
  ISBN 978-1-59555-166-5
  HF5549.5.J63B36 2008
  650.1—dc22                                                    2008031659

*Printed in the United States of America*
08 09 10 11 12 QW 6 5 4 3 2 1

On a daily basis I meet people who feel overworked, overwhelmed, and under-paid, but who are committed to making the changes they need to create stability, success, and abundance.

I dedicate this book to all of you who have shared your stories with me and told me how you have used my books to change your financial destiny. Your courage and success inspire me to continue my life's work: to help people use financial success to express their full potential and live their life's purpose.

# Contents

# Foreword

While many of us can get excited by the initials of our dream team alma mater, USC or BYU or UTA, for example, the truth is that the jersey most of us are wearing would read "OOU," which stands for "Overworked, Overwhelmed, and Underpaid."

In this important, heartfelt, and well-researched work, financial planner and master communicator Louis Barajas lays out a step-by-step system for identifying and then remedying the problems that come with today's complex lifestyle.

I was especially taken by the section addressing the need for simplifying one's life. Recently I took a giant Post-it note and placed it on the wall of my office. I took four different-colored markers and wrote out the name of each project I was working on, or that was working on me. The total number came to thirty-eight. No wonder I, too, was feeling overworked, overwhelmed, and underpaid! So it was with great gusto that I devoured Louis's manuscript, knowing him to be a genius at helping simplify priorities, as well as establishing systems for decision making.

Peter Drucker said the new knowledge worker has it harder than the former assembly-line worker in that assembly-line workers know, or knew, exactly what they were supposed to do. However, today's knowledge workers not only have to execute the work plan but also dream it up. This puts extra pressure on brains that were not designed to multitask at the level we are being driven to do today. I read somewhere recently that trying to accomplish more than three things at the same time leads one to the performance level of someone on drugs. We are so driven by our "to do" lists that we have forgotten our "to be" lists.

"To be, or not to be, that is the question," wrote William Shakespeare. That phrase is now the question for our working society.

I agreed to write this foreword because Louis has demonstrated to me, and to so many others, not only a genius level of performance when it comes to financial planning but more importantly, perhaps, the demonstration of his life—to his family, his community, and his friends.

Every author pours time, energy, and thought into their work, but what Louis Barajas offers us in his latest book is a gift of wisdom, wonder, and, ultimately, love.

Laurie Beth Jones, author of
*Jesus, CEO; The Path;* and *Jesus, Life Coach*
February 14, 2008
San Diego, CA

# Introduction

In 1991, I founded a financial-planning business in the barrio of East Los Angeles. Most of my clients were Latinos who made modest amounts of money but had the same need for good financial planning and education as people with millions in the bank. It was in the barrio that I first saw how stress affected 90 percent of workers. Over and over again I heard people tell me they felt they were working too many hours, there was always too much to do, and they were not adequately compensated for their efforts. Like most financial advisers, I believed that good financial planning and more income would help relieve the financial stress my clients were experiencing.

In 2003, I wrote a book called *The Latino Journey to Financial Greatness*—a manual for helping Latinos (many of whom had minimal access to information about finances) overcome their limiting cultural beliefs about money and develop a plan to create greater prosperity. The book discussed basic financial-planning components and showed readers how to recognize financial predators in their communities. Knowing that most of my intended readers had limited resources and access to bookstores, my marketing plan was to attract sponsors who were interested in using my book to introduce or build their brands in the Latino community. Soon Fortune 500 companies like Sears, Nationwide Insurance, JP Morgan Chase, Bank of America, and DaimlerChrysler contacted us. With their support, over the last several years I have done hundreds of presentations, workshops, and media interviews throughout the country and talked with thousands of Latinos who had never been exposed to financial planning before.

However, during those tours I noticed that the people behind the scenes—media personalities, the staffs of the Fortune 500 companies sponsoring me, and the public-relations people representing those companies—would comment that they felt more stressed than the people in my workshops. I heard the same thing from executive directors and the staff of nonprofit organizations that teach financial literacy. It didn't really matter how much people were making, or the jobs they held. In almost every circumstance, economic bracket, marital status, job title, or length of employment, individuals across the United States reported feeling overworked, overwhelmed, and underpaid.

During this time I also became the first member of a minority to be elected to the national board of the Financial Planning Association, which promotes the value of financial planning and advances the financial-planning profession. While on the board, I had discussions with respected financial professionals throughout the country about what I was accomplishing with the working poor. I soon realized that the manner in which my firm practiced was very different from the norm. We offer financial planning with a human focus, one that serves average Americans who are struggling not only with their finances but also with their lives. Rather than fixating on the size of a client's bank balance, investment portfolio, or retirement account, our approach has always been to devise plans that show clients how to live better lives today, tomorrow, and in the future. This humanity-based wealth planning works well for clients whether they are making $50,000 or $500,000 or $5 million, because everyone has similar feelings and desires. The ways we choose to experience those feelings and fulfill those desires will make the difference between feeling successful or stressed.

I am a financial planner, and my expertise is in helping others use their assets of time, money, and talents to create happier lives. That's why this book focuses on how you can use your time, money, and talents to their best effect. Is money a component of a better life? Absolutely. But so is job satisfaction, spending time with your family, using your skills and strengths to their highest degree, living according to your values, and feeling as if your life makes a difference. And when you spend just a few minutes cleaning up any old, bad beliefs, getting clear on your life priorities, and setting plans in place for your life, work, and finances, then you will find that instead of feeling overworked, overwhelmed, and underpaid, you will start to feel two very different emotions that are the hallmarks of true success: happiness and gratitude.

*Overworked, Overwhelmed, and Underpaid: Simple Steps to Go from Stress to Success* is about creating a successful life through the financial planning and coaching tools that I use on a daily basis with my clients. I have designed this book to be highly interactive, and I encourage you to do the exercises, complete the forms, and utilize the tools described in these pages. You can use the forms in the book, download copies of the forms to your computer or handheld device, or complete them online at my Web site, www.louisbarajas.com. (On the Web site you'll also find two valuable bonus chapters—one on developing confidence through achieving goals, and another on simple steps to create a clear financial plan.) This book is for anyone who is frustrated and struggling to express their full potential and live their highest purpose, whatever that is—being the best dad or mom for your children, having enough so you and your family can live comfortably, running a successful business, or something even grander. No matter what your dream, I believe this book can help you create the prosperity and passion to attain it and still have a life in the process. I look forward to hearing your stories as you join the ranks of the *formerly* overworked, overwhelmed, and underpaid.

# CHAPTER ONE

# Overworked, Overwhelmed, and Underpaid: The Trap of Modern Life

In this chapter you'll learn . . .

⇛ how we are working more, doing more, and getting paid less for it than ever;

⇛ the symptoms that will let you know if you are overworked, overwhelmed, and/or underpaid;

⇛ how changing the way you think is the first step out of the trap of being overworked, overwhelmed, and underpaid;

⇛ the key to mastering your life is the three Ms: mind-set, money, and meaning; and

⇛ how to develop the solutions, strategies, and systems that will take you from stress to success.

How much stress are you under these days? Does the idea of your financial future energize you? At work, are you using your talents to their fullest? Is your day filled with organized actions that move you ever closer to your goals while still leaving enough time for exercise, relaxation, family, and friends? Do you feel appreciated and well compensated for the job you are doing? Or like the rest of us, do you go through your days at what seems like hyper-speed, with at least five times more to do than any one person could ever get done, stuck in a job where you feel underutilized and under-compensated, massively stressed, ignoring the activities and people that are important for your health, sanity, and happiness?

Welcome to twenty-first-century America—the land of the trapped and the home of the stressed. Today it seems that no matter what our income or work situation, far too many of us are struggling, living lives of financial desperation. Desperation exists in neighborhoods where people drive nice cars, live in good-sized houses, take great vacations, and send their kids to private schools, but they are only a paycheck away from bankruptcy. We see desperation in couples where husband and wife each work two or three jobs just to make ends meet, or in single parents who feel trapped between providing financially for their children and spending time with them. Saddest of all, we see desperation in the people who start out with big hopes and dreams, only to wake up twenty years later realizing that time and life have passed them by. They've spent their years occupied with unfulfilling work that kept them from realizing their dreams or spending time with their family and friends.

As a Certified Financial Planner™ and an expert in humanity-based wealth planning, I have consulted for clients with incomes between tens of thousands and tens of millions of dollars, people with negative net worths and multimillionaires, blue-collar and white-collar workers, tradespeople and CEOs, and everyone in between. Most of them have walked into my office or talked with me at a presentation and described themselves with the same three words: *overworked, overwhelmed*, and *underpaid*.

Given what's happened in the United States workforce over the last quarter century, that's not surprising.

## We are working more . . .

» According to information presented at the 1999 National Institute for Occupational Safety & Health Conference, people in the United States work approximately eight weeks longer per year than in 1969, but for roughly the same income (after adjusting for inflation).

» In 2002, women worked an average of 43.5 paid and unpaid hours per week, an increase of 4.5 hours since 1977. Mothers worked a little less, 41.2 hours. Men worked 49 paid and unpaid hours per week on average. Fathers actually worked longer: 50.4 hours per week.

» As of 2002, 78 percent of married workers were dual-earner couples (that is, both partners work). Together, dual-earner couples work an average of 91 hours per week—an increase of 10 hours per week since 1977.

» Nearly one-half (45 percent) of workers with families state that their jobs interfere with family life either "some" or "a lot." One-third (33 percent) of workers are in contact with work once or more a week outside normal work hours. In a 1998 "Family Matters" survey by the National Partnership for Women & Families, 70 percent of working fathers and mothers reported they didn't have enough time for their children.

» Americans work more hours per year than workers in any other country except New Zealand, according to the Organization for Economic Cooperation and Development (OECD).

» One in three U.S. workers—33 percent of the workforce— report feeling overworked as a chronic condition.

» According to a 2000 survey by the Radcliffe Public Policy Center with Harris Interactive, 70 percent of men ages 21 to 29 and 71 percent of men ages 30 to 40 report that they want to spend more time with their families and would sacrifice pay to do so.

» In a 2002 administrative staffing study, 32 percent of workers cited work-life balance as the top priority in their careers, followed by job security (22 percent) and competitive salary (18 percent).

## We feel overwhelmed . . .

» More than one-half (56 percent) of employees say they often or very often (1) have to work on too many tasks at the same time, and (2) are interrupted during the workday and feel overworked and overwhelmed as a result.

» More than one-fourth (26 percent) of the American workforce does not take a vacation each year, and 46 percent of the workers who do feel overwhelmed by the work awaiting them. They talk about feeling as if they are "drowning" in accumulated work.

» The amount of time couples spend with their children on workdays has increased over the past twenty-five years, to 6.2 hours. What this means is that parents have less time for themselves—dads average 1.3 hours each day (down from 2.1 hours in 1977, and moms average *less* than an hour (0.9 hours, versus 1.6 hours in 1977). Is it any wonder families feel overwhelmed?

## We are falling further behind financially . . .

» Since 2001, real hourly wages rose only 3 percent for the middle-income worker, with none of this progress occurring after 2003.

» Every year, about 43 percent of American families spend more than they earn.

» Americans carry more than $700 billion in debt on bank credit cards and retail cards. At any one time, the average household has approximately $8,000 in credit card debt. In 2007, the delinquency rate for credit card accounts reached highs not seen in three years.

» According to statistics from the Federal Reserve, as of November 2007 American consumers owed $2.505 *trillion*, an increase of over $64 billion in one year. That total does not include mortgage debt.

✻ ✻ ✻

Let me introduce you to two people who are "poster children" for this problem. Recently Marie and Jim came to my office in Southern California, to do some financial planning. Jim is a junior high school science teacher, and Marie works as a manager for a construction company. They have a daughter, and Jim is paying child support for a son from his previous marriage.

Marie and Jim arrived thirty minutes late for their appointment. They rushed in with many apologies; there had been a problem with after-school care for their daughter, and they'd had to drop her off at Marie's mother's house. Jim's car was in the shop that day, and Marie had been stuck at the office with a work issue, so they'd left later than they planned. To top it all off, the interstate had been backed up for more than five miles.

When they finally sat down in my office, Jim was grumpy and Marie tight-lipped. I asked them why they had come to see me. Jim started to talk about saving for retirement and the kids' college education, but Marie interrupted him.

"To tell the truth, Louis, what we'd really like to do is leave L.A., move to the outskirts where homes are less expensive, and see if we can get our lives back," she said grimly. "We're both spending way too much time at work, and I feel like half of my work is just pushing paper rather than managing. And even though I've taken on a lot more responsibility at my job, I'm still getting paid the same. Jim's paycheck as a teacher has always been low, so we're managing to get by but not putting anything aside for a rainy day, let alone retirement or college."

Jim nodded. "I like my job and don't want to leave teaching, but we just never seem to have enough time or money. The only time we spend with our kids is when we're driving them to after-school or weekend activities. We get home and fix dinner, and then I grade papers while Marie works on her company's books. We both fall into bed at midnight exhausted. We haven't had dinner together or gone to a movie in months, much less taken a vacation. We want out of the rat race!"

Marie and Jim are typical of the middle-class people we think of as overworked, overwhelmed, and underpaid. But over the years, I have discovered this kind of stress is no stranger to the "McMansion" or the executive office. As an author and financial expert, I work with several Fortune 500 companies that sponsor my workshops in financial education and planning for underserved populations. I've been able to spend time with upper-level executives as well as the heads of public relations firms, professionals in the news media, and officers of many nonprofit organizations. Whenever I mentioned that I was working on a book about being overworked, overwhelmed, and underpaid, people of all income levels would say, "That's me!"

One very successful woman, Susan, head of a PR firm, lived in Texas with her husband and two daughters. The previous year, she'd been recognized as one of the top female entrepreneurs in her area. She had a staff of ten young go-getters and a stable of high-profile clients—yet she told me she felt as overworked, overwhelmed, and overpaid as the people in my seminars.

"I'm working all the time and making six figures, but I'm feeling a lot of pressure for traveling so much," she said. "I can't spend time with my husband and daughters. My job seems to be mostly putting out fires rather than doing the things I really enjoy. I find myself thinking, *I'm not getting paid enough to do this!* And it's not just me—it's everyone in my firm. When we get together at lunch, all we talk about is being overworked, overwhelmed, and underpaid."

Even those fortunate individuals at the level where you would think they "have it all," don't. I recently read an article about the highest-ranking executive producer for a national news program. She's in her early forties, single, at the absolute top of her profession, and well paid—but she talked about working long hours, feeling overwhelmed, and having no life outside of work. "I don't know if this job is worth giving up my life," she admitted.

No matter what your current income or job level, perhaps you, too, are one of the millions who go through the days, weeks, months, and years feeling stressed and dissatisfied, working too much and getting paid too little, but with little or no clue of how to change it. See which of the following statements apply to you:

*You are overworked if . . .*

⇒ You always work more than forty hours per week.
⇒ You haven't taken a vacation in the past year. Even if you do

take a vacation, you can't relax because they are always calling you for an emergency, *or* you feel guilty for not calling to check in.

⇒ You feel that your boss/co-workers/clients don't appreciate your efforts.

⇒ Because of work, you have missed more than one important event with your family (recital, sports, church, etc.).

⇒ Your family doesn't understand when you tell them you don't spend time at home because you are working hard for them.

⇒ You've thought about quitting at least once in the past month.

*You are overwhelmed if . . .*

⇒ It seems that the more work you accomplish, the more work there is. You've missed at least one major deadline in the past six months.

⇒ You don't have enough time to spend with your family and friends. You and your spouse always intend to have a date night, but a work or home emergency always seems to come up whenever you make plans.

⇒ When you think of everything you have to get done, you feel tired or anxious.

⇒ Your stress level has affected your health. You keep putting off visits to the dentist or optometrist because you don't have the time (or money) to go.

⇒ You're always putting out fires and never fully preparing for anything.

⇒ You feel that you are working harder than ever just to stay
even.

*You are underpaid if . . .*

⇒ You put in a significant amount of unpaid overtime.
⇒ You feel more stressed about finances than you did five years
ago. You sometimes have bad dreams or nightmares
concerning your finances or your work.
⇒ Your work doesn't utilize your talents and abilities to their
fullest extent.
⇒ You are doing more work today and getting paid less for it,
*or* you don't feel you are compensated well enough for the
level of work you provide.
⇒ You start saving money for an important goal, but you
always end up spending it on some unexpected emergency.
⇒ No matter how much you make, you can't get ahead
financially.

When you are overworked, overwhelmed, and underpaid, it is as
though you are in a tiny box with walls composed of fear, complexity,
confusion, and frustration. All you can do is beat on the walls or walk
from one side of the box to the other, since it's better to have the illu-
sion of progress than no movement at all. But here's the truth: you're
in a box of your own making, and pacing around inside the box isn't
going to get you where you want to go. In the next three chapters
you'll find specific tools and techniques to help you go from being
overworked, overwhelmed, and underpaid to being balanced, in con-

trol, and well compensated for meaningful work. But these tools and techniques require that you first change the way you think and feel. Once you do so, the changes you wish to make in your work, your time, and your priorities will be a lot easier than you may believe at this moment.

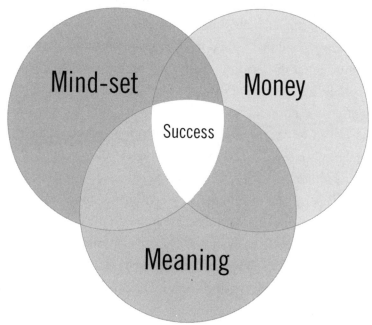

**Mind-set, Money, and Meaning**

Going from stress to success in your finances and your life starts with internal changes, not external ones. The first area where you must put your efforts is the one between your ears. Do you know (or have you read about) people who have very few resources, yet they are immensely happy? Or others who work fifteen-hour days, love what they do, and still manage to have a great family life? I believe it's because they are rich in internal resources. They have mastered what I call the three Ms: *mind-set, money,* and *meaning.*

You can know all the things you need to do to change, but unless you have the right *mind-set* you won't believe you can do them. You have to believe that change is possible, and that making changes will help you be happier, more fulfilled, and more successful. Through the years I have found that I could try to teach people about financial success, but unless they had the right mind-set they wouldn't be able to absorb the information. Most of this book is focused on helping you develop the right mind-set to be able to move from stress to success.

The second M is to understand that your beliefs about *money* will dramatically affect the level of success you will allow yourself to have. Each of us has beliefs about money that either support us or prevent us from taking care of what we have and earning more. All too often our beliefs hold us back. If you believe money is the root of all evil, for instance, then subconsciously you'll end up sabotaging your efforts to become wealthy. If you believe that money is the be-all, end-all, then you'll spend your life chasing money, instead of realizing that what you really want is what you believe money will give you—security, significance, approval, and friendship. And if you don't feel you're worthy of the money you make, then you're likely to ask for less than your work is worth and resent it when you're not paid as much as you deserve. Your beliefs about money will determine how happy or conflicted you are about your wealth or lack of it.

Overworked, Overwhelmed, and Underpaid

The third and final M is *meaning*. What's the difference between someone who feels overworked, overwhelmed, and underpaid and someone who describes life as fulfilling, exciting, and happy? The difference is what we make things *mean*. Have there been times where you were working long hours and you came home feeling tired yet exhilarated? Have there been times when you had a lot of tasks to accomplish yet you felt extremely productive? And have there been times when you put in a lot of hours that you weren't paid for—volunteer work, for example, or supporting your children's school activities—yet you felt well compensated? Meaning provides the inspiration and motivation to put in the work that is important to us. The meaning we attach to our circumstances determines how we feel about our lives, and this ultimately determines both our results and our level of fulfillment. Mind-set, beliefs about money, and meaning are three of the components that have created your current feelings of being overworked, overwhelmed, and underpaid. Even though there are many strategies for changing the circumstances that contribute to your feelings, to move out of stress and into success, you must start by changing your inside first. Throughout this book we'll be working with all three elements to show you another way.

## How to Go from Stress to Success

When I work with small business owners, we figure out what they need to focus on in order to be successful, then create *solutions* for any challenges, and finally develop *strategies* and *systems* that will help them implement those solutions automatically. The same thing applies if you are feeling overworked, overwhelmed, and underpaid. You must

(1) figure out what you need to focus on, (2) find the solution both for your emotions and your circumstances, and finally, (3) develop the strategies and systems to take you out of stress and help you create greater success.

I've given you examples of people who were caught in the overworked, overwhelmed, and underpaid trap. Now let me give you two examples of people whose lives are more fulfilling. The first is my father. For thirty years he owned his own ironworking business in the barrio of East Los Angeles. He worked hard through the years, and there were times when he, too, worked too many hours for little money. But he always made his family and friends a top priority. He was an honorable businessman and gave his clients great value for their money. He had several employees whom he loved and who loved him. At night, he would come home worn out from his labors but happy with the work he had done, feeling loved and cared for by his wife and children. When my dad decided to retire, he gave the business to the employee who had been with him the longest. Over the years, my dad had invested in several residential properties, and my parents now live on the income from their real estate. They still occupy the same house in East Los Angeles and have the same modest lifestyle. They enjoy traveling and being with their children and grandchildren.

My father's income was never large, but it was always enough to support our family. He sees people in his neighborhood or on the TV who talk about being "burned out" and working eighty hours a week, and he shakes his head. "Why do they do that, son?" he asks me. "Life's too short." My father is a wise man who has always been clear about who he is, what his strengths are, and what is important to him. He has lived his life according to his values, and even though he is not wealthy, he is a very happy and successful man.

The other example is myself. At various points in my career I, too, have found myself in the trap of feeling overworked, overwhelmed, and underpaid. I ended up getting a divorce from my first wife because I got caught up in the drive for professional success at any cost. And when I started my financial-planning business in the barrio and earned a grand total of twelve thousand dollars the first year, you'd better believe I felt underpaid! That is why I have spent the last twenty years developing the focus, solutions, strategies, and systems that have helped my clients and me to go from stress to success. I have learned that each of the three feelings—overworked, overwhelmed, and under-paid—have very specific antidotes, and I have discovered and fine-tuned certain tools that I have used with people at all levels of success. These tools can help you leave feeling overworked, overwhelmed, and underpaid behind forever and build a strong foundation for a successful life.

Most of us live unfocused and unbalanced lives. It's like being on a long road trip. Have you ever been driving along the interstate and all of a sudden you think, *Where am I? How long have I been driving?* It's quite easy to get hypnotized by driving mile after mile and forget why you're taking the trip in the first place. At that point you need to pull into a rest stop where you can stretch, take a breather, get a cup of coffee, look at the map, and figure out where you are and what you should do next. That's what these tools will do for you; they will help you draw a brand-new "map" for your journey from stress to success.

overworked

# CHAPTER TWO

# From Overworked to Living a Balanced Life

In this chapter you will discover . . .

⇒ who the most important people in your life are;

⇒ where your energy is going—and where it's not going;

⇒ the secrets of people who successfully balance work and family; and

⇒ a life blueprint that will get you out of being overworked and into real living.

Recently a man, Richard, came to my office. He wanted to create a financial plan so his wife and three children would be taken care of if anything should happen to him. "My father died when he was only fifty years old," Richard told me. "I'm forty-eight and want to make sure all my affairs are in order."

"That's one of the best gifts you can give to your family," I said. "But how about planning for your life as well as your death? How much time are you spending with your family right now?"

Richard shrugged. "My work takes up every waking minute. I'm at the office by 7 a.m., and I don't get home until 8 p.m. at the earliest, and I take work home to boot. On the weekends I try to catch up on paperwork and e-mails. I've always got at least five projects I'm either supervising or working on, and the deadlines are really tight. Two of my best employees quit due to burnout, and their replacements aren't up to speed, so I'm doing some of their work as well as my own. My health's affected, I'm gaining weight, and I'm completely out of shape. My wife's almost as busy with her own job as I am with mine—we haven't spent time together in months. I only see my kids on weekends when they play soccer. And I've got my BlackBerry with me even then."

I took out a sheet of paper and drew a stick figure, a horizontal line, and a rectangle underneath it. "This is you," I told Richard, pointing to the stick figure. "This [pointing to the rectangle] is your ultimate destination—a box, six feet under. That's where your dad ended up at age fifty, and you're now forty-eight. If you were going to end up six feet under in less than two years, how would you spend your time?"

Richard looked stunned. Then he said, "I'd be with my wife and children. I'd visit my parents and brothers and sisters. I'd scuba dive off the Great Barrier Reef in Australia. I'd go out and help people. I'd go to church. I'd try to create special moments for my family to remember when I'm gone." He smiled. "That's a lot more important than just a financial plan," he said.

# The Trap of the Omnipresent Job

Richard is the perfect example of the trap of overwork. In the United States we're told that success at work equals success in life. If we don't do well professionally, we're a failure. And today, with global competition and ever-growing demands to do more in less time with fewer resources, most of us are afraid that we're going to lose our jobs unless we keep up with and even exceed expectations. So we carry our cell phones and PDAs and check e-mail at every hour of the day and night. The forty-hour workweek is for slackers; on average, we are working anywhere from forty-three to sixty hours a week and letting our vacation time accrue because we can't leave the office for too long.

Over the last two decades, American workers have been clocking more and more hours on the job, and they now work more hours than workers in any other industrialized country. According to some studies, 40 percent of employees work overtime every week or bring work home at least once a week. In 2001, the Families and Work Institute reported that 63 percent of all employees want to work less, up from 46 percent in 1992. And a 1998 study by the National Partnership for Women & Families said that 70 percent of working parents felt they didn't have enough time for their children.

It's been shown that the health and performance effects of being overworked are very detrimental. Overworked employees report a higher level of stress and negative effects on their health from their job. They are more likely to experience clinical depression, not to take care of themselves, to make mistakes at work, and to feel angry at their employers. A 2000 Integra Survey stated that 62 percent of workers routinely end the day with neck pain, 44 percent with strained eyes, 38 percent with hand pain, and 34 percent report difficulty in sleeping due to work-related stress. Is it any wonder that, by 1999, 57 percent of business students in eleven countries told PricewaterhouseCoopers that attaining work-life balance was their top career goal? It's also no surprise that fewer employees in the U.S. workforce say they want to seek advancement opportunities on the job because they are overwhelmed by the workload in their current positions.

I know the overwork trap from the inside out. When I started my financial-planning business in 1991, I worked incredibly long hours. I can remember coming home late one night and my own dog barked at me as if I were a prowler. I neglected my family to the point that my wife and I divorced. My health suffered; I gained about thirty pounds, and my blood pressure went up. I've seen the negative effects of overwork up close—enough to make sure to never get caught in the same trap again.

Overworked people become caught up in the urgent demands of one area of life and neglect other aspects that are more important for long-term success—areas like health, family, friends, intellectual and spiritual pursuits, recreation, contribution to others, and many more. If life could be represented as a wheel, with the different components forming wedges, it would look like the chart on the next page.

This represents a typical graph for someone who feels overworked. The biggest part of their wheel is work related (70 percent). Next to that is family at 20 percent, other relationships 5 percent, health is 2 percent, recreation 2 percent, and spiritual and intellectual pursuits 1 percent. Looking at this wheel, what kind of "ride" do you think this

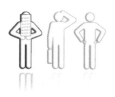

# Life Focus Wheel

**Inner Circle:**
Where are you compared to your ideal outcome?

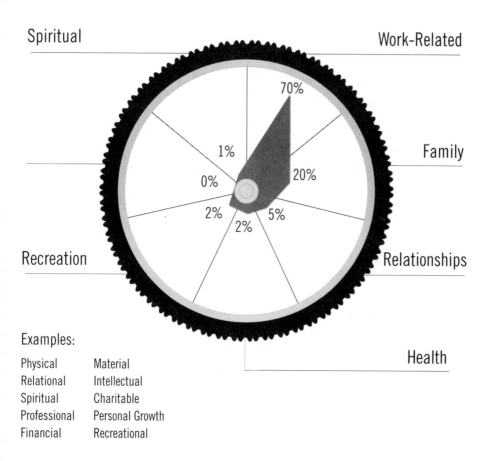

Spiritual               Work-Related

70%

1%              Family

0%    20%

2%    5%

2%

Recreation              Relationships

Health

**Examples:**

| | |
|---|---|
| Physical | Material |
| Relational | Intellectual |
| Spiritual | Charitable |
| Professional | Personal Growth |
| Financial | Recreational |

life would provide? When we are overworked, we forget that we must create some kind of balance in order to have a fulfilling life.

My divorce was the push I needed to take a good, hard look at myself and decide whether I wanted to keep being caught in the overwork trap. I reprioritized based on what was truly important. I worked less but enjoyed my life more. The lessons I learned have allowed me to design a work life that is successful, fulfilling, and balanced—most of the time. I still can find myself working too many hours and taking on too many projects, but now I check myself frequently to make sure I am living according to my own design rather than merely reacting to the demands of the workplace.

There's nothing wrong with dealing with things that are urgent. The problem is that most of us never get around to the things that are far more important to the ultimate quality of our lives. Like saving for retirement. Like spending time with our kids when they're growing up. Like keeping our relationships strong. In today's world, we are guaranteed to have more demands, not less; more work, not less; more competition, not less. Only when we have a clear set of priorities and commit to live by them will we be able to keep the forces of overwork at bay and continue to live a truly successful life.

## The Ultimate Perspective

Imagine it's a beautiful spring day, and you're going somewhere special. You walk into a tastefully decorated room, with thick carpet and plush drapes. Soft music is playing in the background. You see that all the people you know and love are here. Then you notice a coffin against one wall. You walk over and look inside—and see yourself.

You're at your own funeral! Everyone sits down, and then one by one, the people who were closest to you stand up and talk about you. They are completely honest; they reminisce about your good and bad points, every detail of your life, including how they felt about you. Your spouse talks about the years you spent together and how much they meant. Your children share magic moments you created with them and talk about the wisdom you imparted to them over the years. Some of your colleagues stand up and talk about how you made work a pleasure. Then a man in clerical garb talks about your contributions to the community and how your faith played a key part in your life. Finally, your best friend stands up and tells several funny stories about the times you shared over the years and how much it meant to be your friend. You feel grateful to all of them and satisfied that your life had meaning and purpose.

Now, imagine a slightly different funeral. This time there are only a handful of people in suits sitting in the front row. Your family is there, but they look like they want to get away as soon as possible. A man from the funeral home stands up. He says, "We're here to celebrate the life of . . ." and he looks down at the card to read your name. "Does anyone want to say anything?" After a moment of silence, one of your children says that you always worked hard to provide for your family. Someone from your workplace says that they always knew where to find you because you never seemed to leave the office. Your boss agrees: "Best worker I ever had," he says. There's a long, uncomfortable moment, then the funeral director signals for the music to begin. Your family leaves the room quickly, followed by the other mourners. The celebration of your life has taken less than fifteen minutes.

If your funeral were held tomorrow, how would people describe your life? If you die twenty years from now, how would you like them to talk about your accomplishments, your relationships and what you contributed? I once heard someone say, "You never see a U-Haul behind a hearse." When it comes time for your "final accounting," will you really care how many hours you worked, how many promotions you received, how well your business did, or how much money you made? It's very easy to get caught up in today's busyness and fail to spend the time focusing on our ultimate destination. As I once heard someone say, "If the devil doesn't make you bad, he makes you busy." It's only when we are reminded very dramatically of this truth that we take the time to examine our priorities and perhaps change the direction of our lives.

Our perspective at the end of our lives may be very different from when we were in the middle of our careers. It is a good idea to always start with the end in mind, to take a few steps back and, to evaluate where our lives are going today rather than waiting until years from now and regretting our choices. How do you want to live? What do you want to be remembered for? Only when you decide what's really important in your life can you discover a career that's part of your life rather than the other way around. And before you're planted in that cemetery plot, you'll be grateful for what your career has given you instead of regretting what you paid for it in time, money, and effort.

## "Dual-Centric" People Are Happier

You would think that making work your first priority would lead to greater effectiveness on the job and less overwork, but that's simply not true. In 2002, the Families and Work Institute (FWI) published a groundbreaking study of workplace stress in America. As part of their survey of executive men and women in ten multinational companies, FWI asked two questions: (1) In the past year, how often have you put your job before your personal or family life? (2) In the past year, how often have you put your personal or family life before your job? They discovered that 61 percent of respondents put work before family. These executives were classified as work-centric. Seven percent, family-centric, put family before work. The remainder, 32 percent, said that they put the same priority on work and personal and family life. These individuals are considered dual-centric.

Even though you would think that people who focus on both work and family would be more stressed and have less time, according to the FWI survey, *dual-centric people are* less *likely to feel overworked than their work-centric colleagues.* This is true even though dual-centric people work an average of five fewer hours a week than those who are work-centric!

Some other interesting insights into dual-centric individuals:

⇒ *They have the highest ratings for feeling successful at work.*
Dual-centric executive women actually achieve higher levels of success (according to measures like reporting levels, compensation, and number of people supervised) than their work-centric or family-centric sisters.

⇒ *They experience less stress.* Only 26 percent of dual-centric people report moderate or high levels of stress, as opposed to 42 percent of those who are not dual-centric.

⇒ Even though they are more likely to have children under

eighteen still at home (62 percent), *they find it easier to manage their priorities.* While 56 percent of work-centric or family-centric people said it was "difficult" or "very difficult" to manage their priorities, only 31 percent of dual-centric people said the same.

### Four Key Strategies for Creating a More Dual-Centric Life

The authors of the FWI study list four strategies that help dual-centric people cope. You, too, can adopt these strategies and create more balance.

**Strategy #1: *Set strict boundaries between work and the rest of your life.*** When dual-centric people are at work, they focus on work; when they leave the workplace, however, they leave it behind completely. They rarely take work home in the evenings, and they do not make themselves available for work questions or communications outside of working hours. What kinds of boundaries do you need to set to help you separate work and the rest of your life? Could you stop taking work home with you, or if that's too big of a step, could you take work home only one night a week? Could you turn off your cell phone or BlackBerry over the weekend, or check voice mail or e-mail only once a day on Saturday and Sunday? It may take some time and effort to accustom your co-workers to the fact that you aren't always available, but setting clear boundaries will help you be more productive during the hours you are at work.

**Strategy #2: *Focus on whatever you are doing in the moment.*** Have you ever been at work but you were worrying about something at home? Or perhaps you were having dinner with your family but you were expecting a call from your boss, and your daughter says, "I've asked you the same question three times—are you listening to me?" Being physically present does very little good unless you are mentally and emotionally present as well. When you are working, work; when you are with your family, be with your family; when you are relaxing, relax! When you put your full attention on whatever you are doing and are physically, mentally, and emotionally present, you will find that you can give, and gain, the most from the task or relationship.

**Strategy #3:** *Take time for rest and recovery.* Dual-centric people understand that they need to take care of themselves. Give yourself permission to spend time doing whatever helps you renew your energy, even if it's doing nothing at all. When you pay attention to your need for rest and recovery, you will have greater energy and a better attitude at home and at work.

**Strategy #4:** *(This is the most important of all):* **Be clear about your priorities.** When you feel overworked, the reality is that you have lost track of your priorities. You are so busy working in your life that you probably have no time to work *on* your life. As a result, you've forgotten what life is truly about. You must get clear about what is important to you. One of the best ways to do so is to create a "life blueprint" of your goals, roles, values, and key relationships. When you design a blueprint and live it to the best of your ability, you'll feel less stress and more fulfillment—not just on the job, but in your life as a whole.

## Your Plan for a Balanced Life

All of us get caught up in the day-to-day train of life. We keep going along on the tracks in front of us, riding from station to station, and we never think that we can stop, get off the train, and take a look at the route so we can see if we like the track we are on. Instead, we stay on the train as it whizzes by the events of our lives. Before we know it, our small children are in high school and college . . . we've spent ten, fifteen, twenty years on the job . . . we're celebrating our wedding anniversary but there's no passion in the relationship . . . we've lost our hair or gained a set of love handles . . . our lives are almost gone and we've never taken the time to create and live a plan for our lives to ensure we end up happy, successful, and fulfilled. When you reach the end point of your life, will you be proud of the hours you put in at work, or the difference you made in the lives of those you knew and loved? Are you willing to put in a little time planning now so you can create the life and future you truly want?

It's time you got your priorities back on track. To do so, you need to focus on the areas that ultimately have the most *significance* in your life. Is work one of these areas? Perhaps. But when you take a few minutes to examine your life, I think you'll find that work is only one of your priorities, and probably not the highest on your list. Your ultimate goal is to design a life that includes feelings of happiness, success, and fulfillment—not "someday," not "when I make enough money" or "get the promotion" or "sell the business" or "retire rich," but *right now*. And feeling happy, fulfilled, and successful is far more likely when you consciously design a well-rounded plan for your life rather than linking those feelings only to work.

The solution for feeling overworked is to *reconnect with what is truly important to you.* No one comes out of the womb saying, "I want to be the best salesperson or financial planner or store owner in the world!" As children, none of us were interested in cuddling up with a cash register or taking our piggy banks to bed. As teenagers, we may have worked hard at our studies or at sports or at an after-school job, but we wanted other things in our lives too—friends, entertainment, adventure. And after our working days are over, all we will be left with is our lives, so we'd better be sure to fill them with priorities like relationships, education, health, contribution, and pursuits outside of work.

To reconnect with what's truly important, you must utilize two key strategies. First, you must get *perspective* so you can determine what you need to focus on in order to live a happier, more fulfilled, and successful life. Second, you must create a *plan* that allows you to focus on your new priorities and integrate work into a more balanced life.

I'm not suggesting that you have to stop working in order to be happy. Let's be realistic: success and fulfillment rarely come from eliminating work entirely from our lives. For most of us, enjoyable and stimulating work makes us feel worthwhile. (We'll talk about how to make your work more enjoyable and stimulating in chapter 4.) But work must be *one* of your priorities, not the only priority. Your career must be part of your life, not the other way around.

When you've actively created a plan for success and fulfillment, you may be surprised to see where work fits in the design of your life. True success comes from a career that allows you to make the most of your unique abilities, while giving you enough money to take care of yourself and contribute to others, provide your family with a comfortable life, and permit you to spend time creating memories and relationships your friends and family will treasure long after you've gone.

## The Life Blueprint

The system for creating your plan is the *life blueprint*, a tool I created for my financial-planning clients. When clients come to my office, you would think that the first thing we would do together is to examine their current financial resources and figure out how to maximize their returns. But we have found that our clients get better results when they begin with the life blueprint. It's simply a way of discovering what's important to people in every area of life, and of setting goals based on their priorities.

The life blueprint consists of four parts: (1) values, (2) life focus areas, (3) roles, and (4) key relationships. In this chapter you're going to create your own life blueprint as the means of going from over-work to balance. It will take you approximately fifteen minutes to an hour to complete each part. Please allow enough time to go through each part and really think about your answers. Write your answers down, either in this book or in a journal. Don't try to think too much; it's best to rely on your first response. (You might find it easier to do this exercise with a partner asking you the questions, so you can respond not only from your mind but also from your emotions.) Writing things down and actually filling in the charts will give you the kind of concrete plan that you can take and use to create a better life.

## ◇ Step 1: Your Values

Everyone has certain feelings that they want to experience regularly. Love, achievement, success, happiness, growth, security, excitement, and fun are a few examples. The feelings you want will be different from mine, and probably different from your spouse's and your children's. Yet we do what we do, take the jobs that we take, form the relationships that we form, choose the leisure activities that we choose, and so on, because we want to experience these feelings regularly. We call these feelings *values*. If you place a high value on fun, with whom are you going to choose to hang out? People who are fun and who like to do fun things, of course. On the other hand, if you place a high value on responsibility, and your friends want you to call in sick and go out drinking with them, do you think you'll do it? Not likely. Your values determine your actions, your friends, and ultimately the course of your life. The amount of satisfaction and fulfillment you experience is tied directly to how much you experience your values.

We each have a *hierarchy*, an order, to our values. If you value security more than family, and security to you means a steady job, you'll do whatever it takes to keep the job even if it takes you away from your family. If family and relationships are most important, you might actually be happier working less and being with your family more. Knowing the order of your values will help you prioritize the results of your life.

*1. What's most important to me in life?* Think about your current life. What things are important to you? What feelings do you want to experience on a regular basis? Most people come up with anywhere between five and ten values. Here are some examples (in alphabetical order) to stimulate your thinking:

| | | |
|---|---|---|
| Achievement | Freedom | Love |
| Adventure | Friends | Making a difference |
| Being the best | Fun | Marriage |
| Children | God | Money |
| Confidence | Growth | Peace of mind |
| Courage | Happiness | Purpose |
| Creativity | Health | Respect |
| Discipline | Honesty | Security |
| Doing things for others | Humility | Strength |
| Excitement | Humor | Success |
| Faith | Integrity | Teamwork |
| Family | Learning | Wisdom |

If you get stuck, think about the different areas of your life and ask yourself, "Why do I do this? What's important to me about [work, windsurfing, quilting, accounting, bungee jumping, whatever]"? Write down the feeling or emotion you get from that area or activity. For example, my client Richard listed accomplishment, faith, family, security, scuba diving, making a difference, and confidence as his values. When I asked him the feeling he got from scuba diving, he said, "A sense of adventure." So we added adventure to his list.

*2. In what order do these values need to be? What's the most important value on this list?* Put them in order of priority—number one is your most important value, number two the next most important, and so on. Most people can tell their top value fairly easily but may find it tougher to determine which of the lower values is more important than the other. Try comparing one to the other. Richard's

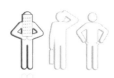

# Values Compass™

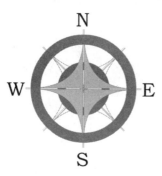

| List Your Top 7 Values in Life | Prioritize Your Top 7 Values (Use a Partner—Don't Judge) |
|---|---|
| 1 | 1 |
| 2 | 2 |
| 3 | 3 |
| 4 | 4 |
| 5 | 5 |
| 6 | 6 |
| 7 | 7 |

top value was security, followed by family, then accomplishment. After that, he hesitated.

"Compare each of the values to the other and ask, 'What's more important?'" I said.

When he compared the remaining values, he determined that faith was more important than confidence, making a difference, or adventure, so faith was number four. Confidence was more important than adventure, and adventure more than making a difference. So Richard's list looked like this:

1. Security
2. Family
3. Accomplishment
4. Faith
5. Confidence
6. Adventure
7. Making a difference

Go through your own list and compare your values to determine which one is more important than the other. Rewrite the list in the new order.

With this step alone, you should start to get more clarity about your life and what's important to you. Most of us discover that while work may help us experience some of our values, it can get in the way of us experiencing all of them. On the other hand, if you are experiencing all of your values at work, then you probably don't feel overworked. When we get to experience most of our values in any particular context, we usually want to spend a lot of our time and energy there. However, that creates another problem. When your life is that unbalanced, you are setting yourself up for trouble. What happens if you lose your job or get into a serious accident? What will happen eventually when you retire from work? If the only place where you get to experience your values is work, how happy will you be when your work is no longer there?

That brings us to the next step in creating your life blueprint. You must identify the major areas of your life that need your attention for you to be successful, happy, and fulfilled.

## ◇ Step 2: Your Life Focus Areas

Imagine that you are at the top of your profession or industry. You're completely fulfilled in your work. Every moment you spend at the office is a joy rather than a job. You're recognized by your peers as an outstanding example of professional success. And then one evening you wake up and find a note from your spouse, who has left you and taken the children. "You haven't been a member of this family for years," the note says. "I hope you enjoy snuggling up to your BlackBerry tonight instead of me, just like you usually do." How would you feel?

Or . . . you wake up in the morning and discover you are completely paralyzed. A doctor comes in the room and tells you that you've had a stroke. The years of eating too much, not exercising, and never going for checkups have caught up with you. You hear the nurse talking about long-term care facilities. You realize the fact that you'll probably never work again is the least of your worries. How do you feel about work now?

A fulfilling life cannot be based upon doing well in only one area. By definition, fulfillment means paying attention to and experiencing your values in several different areas of your life. You can discover your life focus areas by asking some simple questions:

*1. In what areas of life have I been putting my focus?* Here are some examples:

Charitable/Contribution-oriented activities
Finances
Intellectual pursuits
Material (things/purchases)
Personal growth
Physical/Health
Professional/Job/Career
Recreation
Relationships
Spiritual

Write the areas that have been priorities for you, and a few words describing what each area means. Does health mean daily exercise? Eating well? Feeling a certain way? Does relationships include a spouse or partner, children, parents or siblings, friends? If personal growth is one of your focuses, does that include seminars, books, experiences?

*2. How much energy am I putting into each area?* On a scale of 1 to 10, 1 being lowest and 10 being highest, how much time, focus, and energy are you spending in each area? For example, you may feel you're at a 9 in terms of the amount of energy you devote to your career, and your family or relationships area may rate only a 2. (A word to the wise: a rating of 2 in relationships is a good way to end up alone and miserable.) Once you've rated each area, use the Life Focus Area wheel below to write down each area and fill in the corresponding amount of focus you are devoting to it.

 # Life Focus Wheel

Inner Circle:
Where are you compared to your ideal outcome?

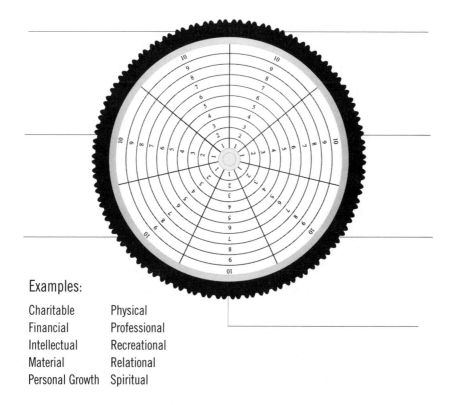

Examples:

| | |
|---|---|
| Charitable | Physical |
| Financial | Professional |
| Intellectual | Recreational |
| Material | Relational |
| Personal Growth | Spiritual |

Now, take a look at your current wheel. Does it represent a fulfilled and balanced life? Would it roll smoothly along the road, or would you experience a lot of lumps and bumps because it's so uneven? Of course, there are certain times when it's appropriate to put more focus on one area or another, depending on circumstances. Parents with a new baby, for example, may focus on the area of family/children. A student may put more focus on intellectual growth. When you are starting a new business or a new job, your career/professional area may require more of your time and energy. However, true fulfillment comes when we learn to develop a balance of time, energy, and focus devoted to the primary areas of our lives. When we design a life plan that allows us to take care of our health, to develop our most important relationships, to have work that is meaningful but not all-consuming, to include time for recreation, contribution, personal, and spiritual growth, then we will feel both successful *and* fulfilled.

*3. Are there areas missing that could cause problems later on?*
Many people pour all their attention and focus into areas like career or family and completely forget that other parts of life need to be priorities as well. Some areas—like health, relationships, and finances—always need at least some of our focus. Other areas, such as recreation, spiritual or intellectual growth, or contribution, may be important to one person and not as important to another. Check your own list and see if there are any areas you need to add in order to design a fulfilling life plan, and rate yourself as to your current focus in those areas.

◇ **Step 3: Your Roles**
Each of us takes on different roles in life. You may be a spouse,

parent, or child; a worker, a supervisor, an employer, or a boss; an athlete, an artist, a student, or a teacher; a colleague, neighbor, friend, leader, teammate, and so on. The amount of fulfillment we experience is directly related to the roles in our lives and how well we feel we are doing in them. Ask yourself these questions:

*1. What roles do I play in life?* Some of these may be very evident—a child or parent or spouse, for instance. Others may be a little harder to discover. Think over the activities of a typical week and ask, "What roles do I fill during this time?" You may be a parent when you get up, an athlete when you go for a jog, a boss when you get to work, a team player during a work project, a community leader in your church, a spouse when you get home, a fan when you watch your favorite team play, and so on. Another way to discover your roles is to look at each of the life focus areas in the previous section and ask, "What roles do I fill in this area?" List all the roles you play in your life on the chart on page 43.

*2. How much energy am I putting into each of the roles in my life?* In the same way you rated the importance of each of your life focus areas, assign to each of your roles a rating of 1 to 10, 1 being the least energy and 10 being the most. Write the number next to the role. Are you happy with your assessment?

*3. Are there roles to which I would like to devote more energy? Are there roles missing that might give me a more fulfilled and balanced life? What other roles would I like to play?* A friend of mine never managed to put enough focus on her physical health. She tried and tried to get excited about exercise, but she couldn't do it.

When she did this exercise, however, she decided to add the role of athlete to her list. Very shortly she noticed that it was a lot easier for her to get to the gym each week. She actually enjoyed working out. She felt more athletic. Eventually she started running and recently completed her first 10K race. Identifying the roles you need to add can contribute greatly to your fulfillment. For instance, many people who experience problems in their relationships after they have children are so focused on the role of parent that they forget the importance of the role of lover. Someone who is promoted at work may have trouble changing roles from teammate or colleague to boss or supervisor. Identifying the roles we need to play in order to experience success and fulfillment is a very simple yet powerful step in your life plan.

William Shakespeare once wrote, "All the world's a stage / And all the men and women merely players / They have their exits and their entrances / And one man in his time plays many parts"—or, as I call them, roles. But unlike Shakespeare's characters, we are the writers, directors, *and* actors in the scripts of our lives. It is up to us as to who we want to be, the roles we want to fill, how much time we spend in each role, and how well or ill we play them. It's up to us whether we play the roles of our lives to deserve polite applause or a standing ovation.

## ◇ Step 4: Your Key Relationships

No one is alone in this world. Everyone has what I call *key relationships*—people who are vital to our success and happiness. Without these people, life would have very little meaning, or would be so difficult that it wouldn't be worth much anyway. To complete your life blueprint, you need to identify your key relationships and how these people fit into your life. Ask yourself these questions:

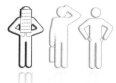

# Roles Revealer™

| List 7 Roles You Act in the Play of Life |
|---|
| 1 |
| 2 |
| 3 |
| 4 |
| 5 |
| 6 |
| 7 |

*1. Who are the most important people in my personal life? What role do I play with each person?* Your key personal relationships might include your spouse or significant other, children, parents, siblings, best friend, pastor or spiritual guide, coach, students, and so on. Make sure you identify each of these people by name, not by the role they fill—"Mary," not "spouse," for instance. Once you have a list of at least seven people, write down next to each name the role you fill with this person. Next to Mary you would write "Spouse" or "Husband," as an example. To your children you would be a father or mother, stepfather or stepmother.

*2. Who are the most important people in my professional life? What role do I play with each person?* Do the same assessment as you did with your personal relationships. The key relationships in your life form the basis of something called your "dream team," which we'll discuss in the next chapter. Your dream team can help you create more success and fulfillment as you help them do the same.

*3. On a scale of 1 to 10, 1 being the least and 10 being the most fulfilled and happy, where am I in each of these relationships? Where do I believe the other person would rate the relationship?* This is a time to be very honest. If you rate the relationship with your children at a 10 and your kids would rate it at a 5, what's the truth? Assess your own level of happiness in the relationship, and then if you're brave enough, ask the other person how he or she feels. After all, both parties have to feel satisfaction with the relationship for things to truly be working well.

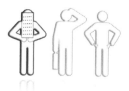

# Relationships
# Recognizer™

| Name 7 People in Your *Personal* Life | What Role Do You Play with this Person? | Name 7 People in Your *Professional* Life | What Role Do You Play with this Person? |
|---|---|---|---|
| 1 | | 1 | |
| 2 | | 2 | |
| 3 | | 3 | |
| 4 | | 4 | |
| 5 | | 5 | |
| 6 | | 6 | |
| 7 | | 7 | |

Congratulations! You have completed your life blueprint. I suggest that you write each of the four areas on a fresh piece of paper so you can see your values, life focus areas, roles, and relationships in one place. It will look like the chart on the next page.

This is the blueprint of your life as it is currently. This process already should have helped you identify parts of your life that need more attention, and parts where perhaps you need to reduce your focus. Here are some suggestions for updating and revising your life blueprint so that you can experience greater fulfillment:

*1. Values:* Which values do you want to experience more of? What changes do you need to make to feel more of this value in your life? If a value is on your list, it's an important feeling; but when you decide you want to experience more of any one value and take action to do so, it can change your life. In going over Richard's list, I asked him which values, if any, he would like to feel more of in his life. He looked at his list and said, "Ten years ago I lost my job and was unemployed for about five months. My wife had to go back to work even though our kids were very young. Eventually I found another job, but it paid a lot less. It took two years for us to dig ourselves out of the financial hole we were in, and five years to get back to the salary I was making before. Now I make really good money, and so does my wife. But I'm always worried I'm going to lose my job. That's why I've been so focused on security, and why I've let myself get so overworked."

"So, what values would you like more of?" I repeated.

He didn't hesitate. "Family and confidence. My family is very

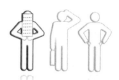

# Life Blueprint Top 7™

| Values | | Life Focus Areas | |
|---|---|---|---|
| 1 | | 1 | |
| 2 | | 2 | |
| 3 | | 3 | |
| 4 | | 4 | |
| 5 | | 5 | |
| 6 | | 6 | |
| 7 | | 7 | |

| Roles | | Relationships | |
|---|---|---|---|
| 1 | | 1 | |
| 2 | | 2 | |
| 3 | | 3 | |
| 4 | | 4 | |
| 5 | | 5 | |
| 6 | | 6 | |
| 7 | | 7 | |

important to me, and I've been pushing them aside because I was so security driven. And I think if I had more confidence in myself, I wouldn't be so worried about money and our future."

"And what new choices would you need to make to have more family and confidence?"

Richard thought a moment. "I'd have to start by taking one day each weekend to focus on being with my family, and I'd ask them to do the same. If we have at least one day that's ours alone, it'll give everyone in my family a sense of how important it is for us to be together. And maybe set up a family dinner one night a week, no matter what. I'll bet my wife and kids would enjoy that as much as I would."

"And what about confidence?" I asked. "What are some things you could do to feel more confident?"

He smiled. "I've been wanting to take an online course covering some of the new technology in my business. That would make me feel like I can keep up with the young people who are working on projects with me. And I'd like to set up weekly update meetings with my boss. Sometimes we feel we're scrambling to keep up with what the corporate executive team is asking for. Checking in with my boss weekly to update her and get the latest information from the executive team would help me build my confidence. It'd also make it easier for me to plan my workload and maybe even leverage some responsibility to other people in my department."

"Would having more of both those values help with your overwork?" I asked.

"Just focusing less on security is a huge load off my mind," he replied. "If I can have more family and confidence, I think I can be more productive at work, even if I'm spending less time there."

Simply by changing your values priority, you, too, can experience more success, happiness, and fulfillment. I suggest you choose at least one value that you would like to feel more frequently, and then come up with at least three ways to add more of that value into your life. Write down those ways and commit to accomplishing at least one in the next week.

2. *Life Focus Areas:* What adjustments do you need to make to create more balance in your life? Which areas need more focus, and where do you need to focus less? Luckily, it can take a very small amount of focus and time in any one area to bring your life back into balance. By exercising thirty minutes a day, three times a week, you can increase your health. By leaving work one hour earlier and taking your spouse to dinner, you can improve the quality of that relationship. By spending Saturday afternoons with your children, you will be astonished at how much closer you will become. (How do children spell love? T-I-M-E.) Decide which area or areas you want to focus on, and then put in the time to bring that area or areas up to par. The idea is to work *on* your life, not just *in* your life. Decide what area or areas you want to focus on, knowing that eventually you will have to put some focus on all areas to attain success.

Richard already had committed to focusing on his relationships area, so we discussed putting a higher priority on his health as well. He decided to start by going to his doctor for a full physical, and then to begin a supervised exercise program to get himself into better shape. He also committed to take his family on a vacation where they could scuba dive. "That's more focus than I've put on recreation in the past ten years," he commented.

3. *Roles:* What roles do you need to focus on more in order to feel greater fulfillment? Which roles do you need to emphasize less? And what will it take for you to reach the level of fulfillment you desire in this role? As a part of this step, you might want to write down a description of how you would be in this role if you were at your best. How could you be the best parent? Best employee? Best contributor to a cause? Best husband or wife or child? Who are you when you are your healthiest? If you're not certain what this would look like, come up with a role model and ask, "What about them made them a great [parent, spouse, boss, athlete, etc.]?" If you want to be better at a role that involves others (like a parent or a spouse), ask the people who would be directly affected how they would like to see you in that role.

Once you've described the role, it may be easier for you to come up with ways to feel more successful in it. Say you rate yourself as a 3 as a spouse because you've been spending so much time at work. You want to be at least level 8. Success to you would mean you spend at least one night a week doing something with your mate—taking a walk, having dinner together after the kids eat, watching a movie, talking, and so on. It also would include a special event with your spouse once a month, just the two of you. If you did those things, you would feel much more successful and fulfilled as a spouse.

If you are feeling overworked in your role as an employee or businessperson, and you're putting a level 10 of time, energy, and focus into this role, how could you reduce that to a level 7, for instance? Maybe you could leave your PDA at work two nights a week and not check messages or e-mail until the next morning. Perhaps you could enlist the support of others to help you prioritize your workload and leverage parts of it. (We'll talk more about that in the next chapter.)

Or perhaps you could simply go out to eat or take an exercise class during your lunch hour so you have a break in the middle of the workday. For each role, come up with ways you can either increase or decrease the amount of focus you devote to it, and ways to feel more fulfilled and successful within it.

Adding to your role doesn't have to be anything big or complicated. In fact, some of the smallest changes can have big impact, both in terms of how you feel in your roles and how other people see you in them. Small changes can be the difference between a role that is an obligation and one that is a joy.

*4. Relationships:* Which of your key relationships do you need to strengthen, and how can you accomplish that? Are there any of these relationships that need to be changed in any way? If you have been caught in the trap of overwork and neglecting your relationships, as part of creating a balanced life you may want to be closer to your children, for instance. Or perhaps if you have been pushing your employees at work very hard to meet a deadline, you may need to put some time and energy into smoothing over any difficulties that arose. Choose at least two personal and professional relationships to work on strengthening, and then come up with at least three specific actions you can take to make those relationships better.

One of the best ways to ensure you will follow through is to share your plan with the individuals involved. Ask them their assessment of the state of the relationship and what they recommend that you could do to make it stronger. Share your plans with them and see if you can enlist their help.

You also may discover that you feel a need to change a relationship because it is no longer serving you in its current form. Have you ever had a good friend or a work colleague whom you've outgrown, or who you just feel isn't good for you? Maybe it's the college fraternity brother who persuades you to drink too much when you go to a football game, or the woman you used to work with who is always furious with her husband and calls you to complain. Perhaps it's a former spouse and you resent the way he or she acted during the divorce. You may need to change the way you relate to these people or end the relationship altogether. Start by asking, "How would I like this relationship to be?" Then approach the other person and ask if he or she would be willing to change the relationship. Ask your fraternity brother if it would be okay if you stopped after one beer. Request that your former work colleague talk about something other than her relationship. With your ex, be clear about how you feel and ask if you both can start communicating with more respect. While none of these actions may be easy, you will find that they may help you create more pleasant relationships with others and reduce your level of stress. In chapter 3 we'll talk at more depth about how to determine which relationships strengthen you, which are your "weakest link," and what to do to create powerful, positive, and supportive relationships throughout your life.

## Life in Business, or Business in Life?

The overworked way of thinking about life and business looks like the diagram on the following page.

For work-centric individuals, the needs of work—whether cash, time, energy, and effort—come first, and the rest of life gets the leftovers. But that's not a recipe for long-term success. Success and fulfillment are more likely to be found among people who understand business is part of life, not the other way around.

The purpose of your career is to give you not just more money but more life, and everyone's definition of "more life" is unique to his or her circumstances and background. But you have to know what's really important to you and what will give you the best quality of life, so that you can decide what you're willing to trade your time, money, and energy for. In my experience, those who prepare a life blueprint for themselves find their careers much more fulfilling because they understand how work fits into the rest of their lives. They feel a greater sense of passion about what they are doing; they can put more of themselves into the time they spend at work while they also take the time for relationships, exercise, worship, community activities, and just plain relaxing. A life blueprint is the secret to both greater balance and greater success for anyone.

I tell a story to my clients about flying from California to New York. Everyone on the plane is going to arrive at the same destination at the same time, but some people sit in first class, some in business class, some in economy, and some are in the back row next to the restrooms with a seat that doesn't recline. You may not be able to change the eventual destination, but you can change the way you travel on the way there. I believe you deserve to fly first class and live an outstandingly successful life. Take the time now to create a life blueprint that can give you that first-class experience. Don't wait for circumstances or the universe or God to remind you how fleeting your life is. Become more dual-centric by using the four strategies in this chapter. And complete your own life blueprint today. Time spent planning your life now will help you experience more fulfillment from now on.

*overwhelmed*

# CHAPTER THREE

# From Overwhelmed to Relaxed and in Control

In this chapter, you will learn . . .

⇒  three key factors that create feelings of being overwhelmed and how to mitigate or eliminate their effects in your life;

⇒  how to identify the 20 percent of work that creates the greatest results, and eliminate the other 80 percent that causes you stress;

⇒  ways to set boundaries and say no effectively;

⇒  the power of building a Circle of Support—a "dream team" to help you simplify your life;

⇒  how to create powerful yet simple systems to streamline your life and attain greater results more efficiently; and

⇒  how to anticipate challenges so you can respond instead of react to them.

The commercials for Staples, one of the big office supply chain stores, feature people in offices where everything is falling apart—copiers breaking, files piling up, people running around or yelling on the phone. Then a woman walks in and says, "Wait! I have the answer!" She pulls out a big, red button with "EASY" printed on it. She pushes the button, and in the blink of an eye, the entire office is transformed: the copier works, files are in order, desks are organized, and people are working efficiently. The boss looks at her and says, "That was easy!"

Wouldn't it be great if we all had an "EASY" button in our lives that would immediately handle our feelings of being overwhelmed and having too much to do? Unfortunately, even though Staples actually sells those big red EASY buttons, we can't cure our feelings of being overwhelmed with it. In the same way we had to look deeper in order to handle our overwork, we need to go broader to eliminate what has caused us to be overwhelmed.

**In the same way we had to look deeper in order to handle our overwork, we need to go broader to eliminate what has caused us to be overwhelmed.**

It seems that more and more of us are caught in the overwhelm trap. One 2001 survey of 1,003 workers found that more than a quarter of them (27 percent) often or very often were overwhelmed by the amount of work they had to do in any given month, and 29 percent felt they seldom had time to step back and reflect on the work they were doing. More and more workers are finding that multitasking and constant interruptions create a lack of focus that can make them feel overwhelmed, uncertain, and unhappy.

Feelings of being overwhelmed can lead to helplessness in the face of current circumstances, and helplessness produces inaction. We look around at everything we have to handle and throw our hands up in the air. We take care of whatever is most pressing—putting gas in the car, for instance—and ignore the things that have more impact on the long term—that oil change we've been postponing for the last few thousand miles. When we're overwhelmed we don't get around to the things that are truly important to the ultimate quality of our lives. Like saving for retirement. Like spending time with our kids when they're growing up. Like keeping our relationships with our spouses strong. We need to reduce or eliminate being overwhelmed so we can focus on our long-term success and fulfillment. When we do so, we will feel more in control of what we do and who we are. Reducing or eliminating feeling overwhelmed is the true "EASY" button for our lives.

## The Three Factors of Feeling Overwhelmed

Being overwhelmed is an indication that your life is out of balance. When you feel overwhelmed, it's usually because of a combination of three factors: *time, resources,* and *complexity.* First, you have too much to do for the amount of *time* you believe you have. For example, a mom who has ninety minutes in the morning to (1) get her kids ready for school, (2) get herself dressed for work, (3) get breakfast for everyone, (4) drive the kids to school, and then (5) fight rush-hour traffic to get to her job on time can easily find herself pushed into feeling overwhelmed if just one thing goes wrong.

One of the most frequent complaints I hear from people who are feeling overwhelmed is, "I just don't have enough *time!*" Indeed, according to a 2002 study by the Families and Work Institute, over 52 percent of workers say that they never have enough time to get things done on the job. Worse yet, 29 percent of employees feel that they put a lot of effort at work into low-value tasks that they classify as a "waste of time."

For most of us, not having enough time isn't just a feeling; it's a fact. As you learned in chapter 1, the 78 percent of workers who are part of a dual-earner couple spend an average of 91 hours a week on the job—11 hours more than a standard 40-hour workweek. But they also spend 6.2 hours each day caring for and doing things with their children. That means over 12 hours each day committed to work or children. In the few leftover hours, dual-earner couples cook, clean, pay bills, do the taxes, try to get organized, and squeeze in a little time together. Dads average a little more than an hour each day for "themselves," and moms average *less* than an hour. Is it any wonder that we constantly feel there is not enough time?

We were told that PDAs and cell phones would save us from having to be at work so long, but those time- and labor-saving devices merely keep us tied to work even when we're at home. And globalization hasn't made things any easier. Nowadays companies are likely to have clients, plants, and even executives working on the other side of the world. You can leave work at night and have fifty e-mails from your offices in China or Europe waiting for your immediate response in the morning. You can be working with a colleague who takes lunch in India at the same time you're going to bed. We are a FedEx/Overnight Express world. Is it any wonder that most of us feel overwhelmed when it comes to time?

The second factor that can cause a feeling of being overwhelmed is a lack of *resources*, or access to them. Your kitchen sink clogs on Thanksgiving weekend, and you can't reach a plumber. Your child knocks out a tooth playing baseball, and you don't have enough money to pay the dentist's bill. You're working hard on a project at the office, but a key team member gets sick and you can't meet your deadline without her. Your boss asks you to put together a report, but he refuses to give you any additional support people to get the job done. In the workplace today we're being asked to do more with less—more work with fewer employees, less time, and less resources—and we're feeling overwhelmed as a result.

Some of us have access to the resources but feel guilty about using them. We feel we should be doing it ourselves, or we believe we don't have the money to pay someone to do it for us. I call this the "rugged individualist" mind-set, and I see it frequently with small business owners. They say things like, "Why should I pay someone when I can do it myself?" or "The only way it'll be done right is if I do it." They refuse to delegate or leverage important tasks to others. These people usually want to keep control of everything, but because they're trying to do too much with too little support, they very quickly feel out of control and overwhelmed. Rugged individualism is a recipe for burnout and diminished returns.

The last factor that contributes to feelings of being overwhelmed is *complexity.* In my profession, every year there are more tools, statistics, and investment opportunities that I need to understand so I can help my clients make the best possible decisions. In our personal lives, with a few clicks we can access an almost infinite range of resources from the Internet: everything from an electrician for the house to a tutor for our children to the latest news and financial advice. That's great—but isn't it harder to wade through all these resources to select what you truly need?

Most of us have reached what Dan Sullivan calls the "ceiling of complexity." Each of us has certain things we're good at and other things that we're not. If you're good at something—numbers, for instance—balancing your checkbook won't cause you to feel overwhelmed (unless you don't have enough money in your account). But people who aren't good with numbers may find balancing a checkbook above their ceiling of complexity. It's also possible to reach a ceiling of complexity in areas where you do have experience. You may feel perfectly competent balancing your checkbook but get overwhelmed when it comes to making decisions about your retirement funds. You may know how to create spreadsheets and customized formulas in Excel, but building the custom reporting software your company needs is beyond you.

Sometimes we can reach our ceiling of complexity simply because we're trying to do too many things at once. In 2004 a report called "Overwork in America: When the Way We Work Becomes Too Much" contained results from a survey of over a thousand wage and salaried workers in the United States. Its findings reveal how much trouble we are having with our multitasking jobs:

⇒ Fifty-six percent of employees said they often or very often (1) have to work on too many tasks at the same time, or (2) are interrupted during the workday.

⇒ Sixty percent who have to work on too many tasks at the same time feel highly overworked versus 22 percent who sometimes multitask.

⇒ Sixty-four percent who are interrupted feel highly overworked, as opposed to 26 percent who are sometimes interrupted.

Here's one of my favorite examples of the effects of multitasking. In 2005, a psychiatrist in London gave IQ tests to three groups of adults. The first group just took the test, the second group was distracted by e-mail and phone calls, and the third group was stoned on marijuana. To no surprise, the first group's average score was ten points higher than the group that had the second-highest score. However, the second-place group was not the people who were distracted by e-mails and phone calls, for their average score was six points *lower* than the people who were stoned. (And I guarantee that the multitaskers didn't enjoy the testing process nearly as much as the stoners.)

Eliminating feelings of being overwhelmed requires the opposite of multitasking. Instead of doing more, you need to do less. Instead of doing things by yourself, you need to create a team. And instead of focusing on broadening the demands on your time and energy, you need to put your efforts toward fewer areas in which you have the chance to excel.

## The Cure for Being Overwhelmed Is to Simplify

When you feel overwhelmed, you need to focus on *simplifying* your situation. The reality is that all of us have finite time, energy, and resources, and all of us have ceilings of complexity. You must decide how and where to put your resources, what you can eliminate, and how you can leverage, delegate, or enroll others to help you achieve your goals. Simplification means that you have to pare down the tasks in your life and eliminate the things that are less important so you can focus on what truly matters.

Most people who feel overwhelmed want to be able to relax yet still feel they have control over their lives. It is possible to go from being overwhelmed to relaxed and in control, but you will need to put effort, energy, and focus into developing strategies that involve *people* and *priorities.* You must focus on the 20 percent that will give you 80 percent of the results you desire. You must learn to set boundaries and say no. You must put together a dream team who can support you and whom you can support. And you must streamline your life by automating as many repetitive tasks as you possibly can.

There are five key systems that will help you in this process. They are the 80/20 List, the Boundary Re-setter, the Dream Team Builder, the Systems Solution Selector, and the Future Response Formula.

## System #1: The 80/20 List

To get out of being overwhelmed, you need to *focus on the most important tasks and areas in your life.* The 80/20 Rule is a time- and business-management principle. It states that 80 percent of our results come from the effort we put into the 20 percent of things that really matter. In my experience, the reason so many of us are overwhelmed is that we are focusing on the 80 percent of tasks that produce very few results. Instead, we should put most of our efforts into the 20 percent of tasks that will make the biggest difference. Instead of "working smart," you are working on the smart things.

How do you know if you're in the 80 percent? See if any of these ring true:

⇒ You focus on what's "urgent" instead of what's important.

⇒ You end up attempting tasks or jobs even though you're

not any good at them, simply because they need to be done.

⇒ You take a lot longer to accomplish things than you anticipate.

⇒ You use the "O" word—overwhelmed—a lot.

⇒ You end up doing things because other people want you to do them, not because you want to.

On the other hand, when you're working in your high-impact 20 percent:

⇒ Your activities help you fulfill your life blueprint.

⇒ You're doing what you've always wanted to do.

⇒ What you do makes you feel good about yourself.

⇒ Even if you don't particularly like what you're doing in the moment, your activity helps you attain your goals.

⇒ You can leverage or delegate the tasks you don't like or aren't good at doing.

⇒ Overall, you feel satisfied with your life and work.

Your goal with the 80/20 List is to identify what needs to go into your 20 percent, and what can be put on the 80 percent that produces fewer results. Then you'll create a plan that allows you to focus most of your efforts on the 20 percent. You create your 80/20 List by making a list of everything you do during an average week, and then asking questions about each task to determine if it should be in the 20 percent or 80 percent. You will use these lists to help you decide what to eliminate, what to delegate, and what to keep as part of your daily life. This exercise should take about an hour, and it probably will be one of the best uses of an hour you could make.

1. Make a list of everything you do during an average week—and I do mean everything. Start with getting out of bed and getting ready for the day, all the way until you get back into bed at night. (Include "sleep" on your list too.)

2. Ask yourself, "What's important to me ultimately? What do I *really* want to do with my life and my time?" (You might want to refer back to the life blueprint you created in chapter 2.) Write a sentence or two on this topic at the top of another piece of paper.

3. With that goal in mind, review your list and ask, "What 20 percent of my actions should I be focusing on to attain that goal? What 20 percent of my activities will give me 80 percent of my rewards?" Write an "I" next to the 20 percent of things that you consider the most important to accomplish in order to feel happy, fulfilled, and successful. For instance, meeting with new clients may be very important for your business, while logging your expenses is not. Picking up your dry cleaning is not important, but having dinner with your family is. Remember, you are only allowed to put an "I" next to 20 percent of the items on your list!

4. Rewrite your "Important" items on the piece of paper where you wrote what you want most in life. This is your 20 Percent List, where you will be focusing most of your efforts.

5. Looking at your 20 Percent List, ask yourself, "Is there anything I need to add to this list that will give me more results?" Up to this point, you've probably been focusing a lot of your energy and attention on the 80 percent that was urgent rather than important. If you didn't have to deal with that 80 percent (and we'll talk about how to do that later), what else could you do that would increase your success and fulfillment? Could you take a class to increase

# 80/20 Focus

| | List Every Activity You Do | I/N |
|---|---|---|
| 1 | | |
| 2 | | |
| 3 | | |
| 4 | | |
| 5 | | |
| 6 | | |
| 7 | | |
| 8 | | |
| 9 | | |
| 10 | | |

your work skills? Take on a new project that will showcase your abilities? Exercise so you'd be healthier and have more energy? Take your kids out for an early-evening stroll? Volunteer with your church? Spend quality time with your spouse? Choose one or two things that would give you the greatest expansion of your results in life, and add them to your 20 Percent List.

6. Look at all the items that remain on your original list—the things that take up 80 percent of your time but give you little to no satisfaction. Of these items, what are the 20 percent you hate the most? If you could eliminate 20 percent of the things on your list with the wave of a hand, which ones would go? Put an "N" next to these items.

7. Rewrite the "N" items on a separate page. This is your "Not-to-Do List." Your goal will be to come up with strategies so you never have to do these things again. We'll return to this list when we talk about systems 3 and 4, the Dream Team Builder and the Systems Solution Selector.

8. Everything left unmarked on your original list is part of the 80 percent that has been draining your energy and resources while providing limited results. Rewrite these items on a new piece of paper, and label this your "80 Percent List." Think how great it would feel to never have to deal with these items again!

Your first goal is to use your 20 Percent List as the guideline for a productive day. I suggest you post copies of your 20 Percent List both at home and at work. Whenever you find yourself feeling stressed and unfocused, look at your list and ask, "Am I working on the 20 percent that's getting me what I want, or am I stuck in the other 80 percent?"

Do whatever you can to bring your focus, energy, and efforts back to the 20 percent. If something isn't going to get done, make sure it's not part of that 20 percent. Whenever you're caught with too many 20 percent tasks, look at each one and ask, "Would I be satisfied if this were the only thing I accomplished today?" It's a great way to build a day that will feel less overwhelmed and more successful.

In *The 4-Hour Workweek*, Timothy Ferriss writes, "Being overwhelmed is often as unproductive as doing nothing and is far more unpleasant. Being selective—doing less—is the path of the production. Focus on the important few and ignore the rest." The 80/20 List will help you refocus your efforts on the tasks and areas that are your true priorities. But your next step must be to eliminate as many of the items on your 80 Percent List as you possibly can. That will take three more systems: setting boundaries, creating a dream team, and streamlining your efforts.

## System #2: Set Boundaries and Learn to Say No

The only way to put focus on the 20 percent and eliminate the 80 percent is to learn to say yes to what's important and no to everything else. You must set boundaries. This is often more difficult than prioritizing for two reasons. First, most of us are terrible at saying no to the demands of others. We need to take care of the kids, spouse, parents, friends, people at church, or volunteer group. Our bosses, clients, co-workers, employees, suppliers, or shareholders put demands on our time, energy, and resources. How can we say no to their needs without seeming selfish? How can we maintain vital relationships if we say no to others' requests?

Second, most of us are subject to what I call "boundary creep." A friend asks you to drop off his dry cleaning when you drop off yours, and it becomes a weekly occurrence. Your son asks you to help out at his Little League game, and somehow you find yourself becoming an assistant coach. You offer to make cupcakes for your daughter's first-grade class, and the next thing you know, you're making snacks every other week. You volunteer to help out with an urgent project at work "just this once," and then it seems as if everyone figures they can dump their emergencies on your desk. All too often we're responsible for the first breach of our boundaries because we want to be nice, or because we can see the need, or because it's important to the other person. But once a boundary is moved, it usually stays moved; and those additional tasks may push us into being overwhelmed.

> We need to stop thinking of boundaries as barriers and start thinking of them as guides that keep us on the road to success and fulfillment.

We need to stop thinking of boundaries as barriers and start thinking of them as guides that keep us on the road to success and fulfillment. Say I wanted to go from my home in Irvine, California, to downtown Los Angeles (about forty miles away). I could take surface streets, with all the stoplights and cross streets and traffic entering the roadway at every block. Or I could take the interstate, which has a limited number of entrances and exits; no cross traffic, intersections, or stoplights; and more lanes heading in the same direction. Most of the time, the interstate is going to get me to L.A. a lot faster than surface streets, simply because it has fewer options to distract me or slow me down. Boundaries work much the same way: they can help you get to where you want to go much faster and with fewer distractions.

You'll also find that setting boundaries—and sticking to them—will decrease your feelings of being overwhelmed and allow you to be more relaxed and in control.

To set effective boundaries, you will need to develop certain skills. First, you must learn to say yes to what will support your true priorities—the 20 percent of activities that gain you 80 percent of your results. Then you must learn to say no in such a way that creates cooperation rather than conflict. Once you learn to say no, you'll find it much easier to say yes to the things that matter because you'll have more time, energy, and resources.

Let's start with your Not-to-Do List (page 75)—the items that cause 80 percent of your stress. You have three choices for these items. First, you can do nothing except complain about them. (I hope you no longer consider this a viable choice.) Second, you can leverage or delegate them. We'll discuss how to do that with the Dream Team Builder system later in this chapter. Third, you can simply say no to doing these things. That may seem to be the easiest alternative of the three, but as most of us realize, saying no can take a great deal of courage. However, if you wish to eliminate feeling overwhelmed from your life, you must learn how to say no effectively.

William Ury is an internationally renowned expert in negotiation and conflict resolution. His books *Getting to Yes, Getting Past No,* and *The Power of a Positive No* are classics. Ury teaches that, in order to say no effectively, you must start with saying yes to what is truly important to you—the priorities you described as part of your life blueprint.

*From now on, every request that you receive for your time, energy, or attention needs to be evaluated based on your life blueprint.* How much easier is it to contemplate saying no to a request from your boss to work yet another weekend when you remember that your relationship with your spouse and children is number one on your values list? Or to refuse to be the leader of your church's fund-raising committee if you look at your list of roles and realize that you need to focus more on being a leader at work? You need to decide what you want to say yes to based upon your true priorities rather than what is urgent in the moment. Evaluating opportunities using your life blueprint will help you to select the ones that will give you more happiness and fulfillment in the long run. Every "no" must arise from your being clear on the ultimate "yes" of your priorities and interests.

Once you have become clear on what you wish to say yes to, you must decide how you wish to say no to the other 80 percent of requests that come your way. Sometimes a simple "No, thanks" will suffice. A co-worker asks you to go to lunch and you're working on a report for your boss. "No, thanks," you say nicely. "Ask me tomorrow when I'm not on deadline." Your best friend wants you to help him with his latest DIY project. You tell him, "No, thanks—I told my kids I'd spend Saturday with them." Or you simply say, "No, thanks," and move on to another topic. You'd be surprised how many requests can be deflected simply by saying no without guilt or explanation.

What about the more difficult no's—the ones where the requester will feel hurt by your refusal, or where there may be consequences to your refusal? We've all had to say no to our kids or our spouses or our best friends; we've probably been stuck telling our boss that we can't take on a particular project, or informing a client that we can't deliver a product by a certain date or can't make the modifications they want or can't meet their price requirements. How can you say no in such a

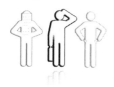

# The Boundary Resetter™

| 20-80 Focus "Not-To-Do" List | |
|---|---|
| **1** | ○ Do Nothing<br>○ Delegate<br>○ Say No |
| **2** | ○ Do Nothing<br>○ Delegate<br>○ Say No |
| **3** | ○ Do Nothing<br>○ Delegate<br>○ Say No |
| **4** | ○ Do Nothing<br>○ Delegate<br>○ Say No |
| **5** | ○ Do Nothing<br>○ Delegate<br>○ Say No |
| **6** | ○ Do Nothing<br>○ Delegate<br>○ Say No |
| **7** | ○ Do Nothing<br>○ Delegate<br>○ Say No |

way that the other person will accept your refusal? Try sandwiching your no in between two yesses: the first yes expresses your interests, and the second yes invites an agreement that takes the interests of both parties into account. In between the two is a clear expression of the boundary you are setting in this circumstance.

Let's take an example from the life of Susan, the woman with her own PR firm whom you met in chapter 1. When we discussed ways to eliminate her being overwhelmed, at the top of Susan's list were calls from a certain client. This gentleman would call at the last minute and request that she schedule new media appearances in the cities where he was speaking. Normally Susan liked to schedule such interviews weeks in advance, to ensure proper positioning and adequate prep time. But because this gentleman was one of her best clients, she had been reluctant to tell him no. As a result, she would work overtime and put pressure on her staff to set up the interviews. She also called in a lot of favors with her media contacts. Every time this gentleman called, Susan could feel her stomach tightening and her head starting to pound. "If I could just get rid of the last-minute stuff, I could do a better job for him, with a lot less stress for me and my staff," she told me.

Susan and I worked to create a way to say no to this client effectively. She called him and began the conversation with a statement of her priorities (her personal yes). "Joe, we need to talk about one aspect of our working relationship. I am committed to do the very best job I can for you in maximizing the media you receive when you're on a speaking tour. It's important to me that you're seen at your best when you go for an interview, and that my firm is also seen as a top-notch professional organization with the media. I want to ensure continuing relationships with media contacts for both you and us."

At this point, Susan expressed her no. "Because of this, we no longer can accommodate your last-minute requests for extra media interviews while you're on the road. It puts a great deal of stress on me, my staff, and my media contacts, and it makes you and us seem less than professional."

Then she ended with a yes that invited agreement on both sides. "I would like to propose that two months in advance of every speaking engagement we set up an expanded media schedule for you in that market. You will know in advance exactly what your schedule will be whenever you're on the road. You and your interviewers will have several weeks to prepare, which will make for better interviews and better PR. I believe this process will be less stressful and more productive for us both."

Joe agreed to Susan's terms, and they set a date to discuss his upcoming speaking tour. It took a little while to train Joe not to make those last-minute requests. The first time he called from the road and asked for a last-minute media interview, Susan told him, "You said you would stick to the schedule we set up and not try to add anything last-minute." Joe blustered a bit, but then agreed. Because Susan stuck to the boundaries she had established, she felt better and was able to do a better job for Joe.

Think about one situation in which you need to say no to someone, and create your own "yes-no-yes" action plan. What priorities and interests do you need to communicate (your personal yes)? What has to change (the positive no)? What agreement do you wish to reach (the yes that invites agreement)? Whenever you need to set or reset boundaries, it's best to plan it out in advance. Saying no can be an emotional moment, and the last thing you need is to be swept up by emotion. Saying no requires calmness, compassion, and confidence. Planning what you want to say in advance will allow you to think through all your options and come up with a solution that will serve your needs as well as the other person's.

A few words of advice: First, be prepared for an emotional reaction. None of us likes being told no. However, you must hold your ground. Persistence and patience will be your best allies in setting your boundaries and staying firm. Keep reiterating your no without allowing yourself to get caught up in what the other person is feeling.

Second, if the other person turns down your invitation to agreement, be prepared to negotiate. She may feel that you haven't taken her needs into account. Ask, "What would you propose?" You don't necessarily have to agree with the proposal, but it's important to hear the person out. Be willing to compromise, but only if the compromise fulfills your interests as well as hers. If the proposal doesn't work for you, say so, and then propose an alternative.

Third, always have an option that will fulfill your needs even if it doesn't involve the other person. In Susan's case, she had decided that the extra stress and work caused by the client's last-minute requests weren't worth it and she was willing to refer him to someone else. Having a fallback position allowed her to be firm in her request to Joe, and ultimately produced the result she wanted.

Saying no may not be easy, but indiscriminately saying yes is a recipe for being overwhelmed. We all need to become comfortable with saying no so we may establish clear boundaries that will support us in achieving the things we truly want. Saying no can leave room for you to say yes to what's truly important.

## System #3: Build Your Dream Team

When I first started my financial-planning business in 1991, I had very limited resources, and, like most small business owners, I figured I had to do everything myself. So I networked, put up flyers, answered the phones, did all the bookkeeping and accounting and filing—and made a total profit of twelve thousand dollars. I worked fifteen-hour days and went home exhausted and overwhelmed.

I knew I needed help, so I focused on the one thing that was driving me crazy: I had no one to answer my phone. I would be meeting with clients and have to interrupt them to take a phone call. I needed a receptionist. I hired a bright young woman who lived in the community and paid her seven dollars an hour, or fourteen thousand dollars a year—more than I had made myself the previous year. But hiring her was the best decision I could have made. Not only did she answer the phones and schedule appointments, but she also took over much of the office work. I could focus on seeing clients and developing new business. I felt much more relaxed and in control of my workday. And even with giving her a raise after six months, I still doubled my personal income that year simply because I made much better use of my time, energy, and resources.

It took one more dive into being overwhelmed for me to really get the "dream team" lesson. Once my receptionist took on much of the office work, I expanded our client list dramatically. Before I knew it, I was back to working insanely long hours because I thought I couldn't afford to hire another financial professional. Luckily, my learning curve was much shorter this time, and I hired another financial planner for around twenty-five thousand dollars a year. This freed me up to expand our marketing efforts to the business community. That year we landed our first big business client, and even though I was now paying two employees, my personal income doubled again. Equally important, I was able to feel relaxed and in control of the business. I had moved from being a rugged individualist to the head of a dream team.

When you feel overwhelmed, you need to build a strong support team to give your career and life a solid foundation. There are people who have the expertise, experience, or time to take something you consider difficult and handle it easily. Remember, your goal is to focus on the 20 percent that gives you 80 percent of your results. To do so, you must build a dream team of supporters to help you along the way. This dream team does not have to be composed of superstars; it is simply all the people in your life who can handle the stuff that drives you crazy. Let me give you a few examples. Say you're working hard on a big project. You look up at the clock and realize that it's 5:55 p.m. You've been so busy that you haven't had a chance to drop your clothes off at the dry cleaner's, which closes in five minutes. But what if one of the members of your dream team was a dry cleaner who picks up from and delivers to your office?

> This dream team does not have to be composed of superstars; it is simply all the people in your life who can handle the stuff that drives you crazy.

Many of my clients are professional women with children. When I ask them about their dream teams, most will list doctors, attorneys, bosses, top producers, and so on. But when I ask, "What's your biggest frustration?" they often say childcare. So I'll tell them, "As part of your dream team you must have people you trust to care for your children. Do you have a babysitter you can call at the last minute? Who's your emergency contact if one of your children gets sick and you're out of touch for any reason? What if you spent an entire day interviewing people, getting someone whom you felt really confident with and who really liked to care for your children? How much less overwhelmed would you feel if there were someone to watch your kids so you could take a bubble bath, or stay late at the office knowing that your children are safe and happy?"

If you are worried about the expense of hiring others to take on tasks you normally do yourself, or you're feeling guilty for not doing certain tasks, do a cost-benefit analysis. How much is your time worth? Wouldn't it be better for you to do what you love and are good at, instead of wasting your time doing things that other people actually may enjoy and/or make a career of?

When I started to get very busy as an author and speaker, my wife, Angie, became my agent and manager as well as my travel and media coordinator. But every weekend she would spend a full day cleaning our house. When I asked why she didn't hire a cleaning service, she said it was her responsibility to keep our home clean and beautiful. "But, Angie, you're doing so much more for me by helping me with my career," I told her. "Besides, housecleaning is taking away from the time you could be spending with our kids and with me." Angie agreed, and we hired a cleaning service to come in every other week. Today Angie's stress level is diminished because she can spend more time being with her family.

To build your own dream team, you must (1) figure out what you need based on the priorities you set with your 80/20 List; (2) figure out who could do it for you; and (3) set up a plan to utilize others as resources. Here's a fifteen-minute exercise to help you get started:

1. Look at your 80 Percent List—the things that take up your time without producing many results. You already should have eliminated some of the items on this list simply by saying no. Cross those items off your list.

2. For each remaining item, ask yourself, "Who could help me with this?" For instance, if you spend eight hours a week preparing meals for your family, could you get help with the preparation from your kids? If you hate filling in expense reports at the office, who could take that task over for you? Next to each item on your 80 Percent List, write someone to whom you could leverage or delegate this task. Even if you're thinking, *They could never do it as well as I do*, or *They'd take too much time*, write down the name or job of someone who could take that task off your hands if you couldn't do it. Include people who are already in your life (your kids, the receptionist at work, your spouse, a friend) and those who aren't yet (a cook, an assistant, a babysitter, a tax preparer, and so on).

3. Choose at least three tasks from your 80 Percent List that you can delegate immediately. You can start with the ones that bug you the most, or with the ones that are the easiest to delegate. If you hate expense reports, hire someone part-time to do them for you. You don't have to spend a lot of money: perhaps your teenage child could organize your receipts and write everything down in order, so all you have to do is total the expenses and sign the form. Once you decide that it's possible for others to take on tasks you don't want to do, you may be surprised at how creative you can become!

Sometimes the best solution is to do something you enjoy in exchange for someone else taking on a task you hate. If you hate having to cook and you know that your neighbor loves it, see if you could babysit her kids every Sunday afternoon in exchange for her preparing two casseroles for your family (you would of course pay for the ingredients). If you're good at figures and your spouse is great at English, then you coach the kids on their math homework and balance the checkbook while your spouse checks term papers and school essays and writes your family Christmas letter. Everyone in life has special gifts—the things they love to do and do well. In the next chapter we'll talk more about how to discover and enhance your special gifts. Once you've eliminated or delegated much of your 80 Percent List, you're free to focus on the 20 Percent List and figure out ways to enlist others in helping you spend more time doing what you love. We'll talk more about this in chapter 4.

In my office we use what we call the Circle of Support to help people represent visually how their dream team can support them. You can use the form on page 85 (or download the form from www.louisbarajas. com), and do the process yourself. You'll use one diagram for your personal life and one for your professional life.

## Your Personal and Professional Circles of Support

1. Write your name in the middle circle of the first diagram, and in the circles around the outside, write all the people who support you in your personal life. Include family and friends, babysitters, doctors, teachers, coaches, and service providers with whom you

have a personal relationship. (The person who reads your electrical meter wouldn't be on your list, but the one who does your taxes every year might be.) For each person, write a few words describing how they support you.

2. On a separate diagram, do the same thing with the people who support you in your professional life—associates, bosses, teammates, accountants, suppliers, clients, and so on. In each circle, write a few words describing how they support you.

3. At the bottom of each page, write all the people you came up with who can help you eliminate the tasks on your 80 Percent List. For example, you might include a dry cleaner who picks up and delivers, a great babysitter, a reliable housecleaner, a computer whiz who can keep your PC running no matter what, a neighbor who helps you with your "Honey-Do" list—whoever would take over the tasks you don't want to do.

4. Finally, look at your 20 Percent List—the things that give you the most results in your life. Who could you add to your dream team to help you get even more results? Are there people in your current dream team who could support you even more with these tasks? Add the new people to your support circles, and under the names of the people you believe could offer you even more support, write what you would like them to do.

Sometimes we have people in our current dream team who aren't supporting us as well as we would like. You may have a CPA you've been using for years, but your finances have become more complex and he or she isn't up to the task. Or one of your in-laws took care of your children when they were infants, but now you'd prefer to put

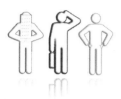

# Dream Team Builder
# Circle of Support™

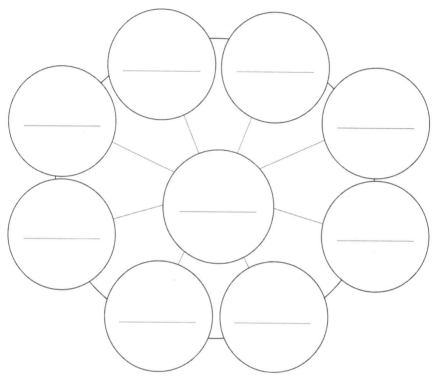

your kids in a day-care setting. Or perhaps you have a friend who likes to smoke and you no longer do unless you're in his company. There's a saying in Spanish that translates as, "Tell me who you associate with and I'll tell you who you are." When it comes to your dream team, you're only as strong as your weakest link. Hard as it may be, you need to ask, "Who's really supporting me at the highest level? Who isn't supporting me? Is there a 'weak link' that I need to either replace or limit my contact with, or at the very least change the rules of our relationship?" With the CPA, for instance, you may need to find someone who has the financial expertise you require. If you place your children in day care, you'll need to change your relationship with your in-law from caregiver to family. And you may need to tell your smoking friend that you prefer to not be with him in settings where you could smoke because you're committed to never smoke again. This is not an easy or comfortable process, and certainly there are some members of your dream team who may be hurt. I suggest you use the "yes-no-yes" process described earlier in this chapter to help you avoid hard feelings while building a team that will support you at the highest level.

On the other side, there may be relationships that you would benefit from deepening. Perhaps you have a professional mentor who has always given you great career advice. Would you benefit from spending more time with him or her? Would you benefit from deepening or adding to your relationship with your spouse or children? When I wrote my first book and began a second career as an author and speaker, both my wife, Angie, and stepson, Eddie, came to work for me. Angie handled all of the speaker bookings, and Eddie built all my PowerPoint presentations. By adding my family to my business, we became closer. Are there relationships that you could deepen by spending more time with these people or perhaps involving them in other parts of your life? Perhaps you could invite your co-workers or boss to help you feed the homeless, or attend the theatre with you, or go to a class to enhance your business skills. Maybe your kids would like to help out in your business. Investing time and energy in deepening relationships is always worthwhile.

Remember, just as you would like each member of your dream team to provide you with outstanding support, you must do the same for them. What kind of support are you providing for your spouse? Your children? Your boss? Your teammates/co-workers? Your clients? Your doctor, attorney, CPA? The person who cleans your house and the plumber who fixes your sink? "Outstanding support" doesn't have to add anything to your list of things to do (which you are trying to pare down dramatically). It does mean that you ask the question, "If I expect X from this person, what will I provide in return?" If you expect your boss to give that overtime project to someone else so you can spend the weekend with your spouse, what can you do to help her out? Can you find additional resources, gather a team to support her, come in early on Friday so you can get things in order before you leave for the weekend?

If you want the best service from the professionals you employ, there are two important ways to provide support. First, say thank you. Recognition and sincere thanks for a job well done are some of the best support you can give. Second, tangible acknowledgment will show many professionals that you appreciate their going the extra mile for you. This can take the form of a bonus, a gift at holiday time, a letter of praise sent to their boss or employer or other clients, and so on. Referrals are also a great way to let them know they are doing an outstanding job.

> When you learn to let go and allow others to help, you'll find that your feelings of being overwhelmed will subside and you'll be able to focus on the things that make your life fulfilling and successful.

People are put in front of us to help us, and vice versa. If you feel overwhelmed, it may be because you're not utilizing your dream team to its fullest advantage. Your dream team is there to help you succeed by allowing you to follow your passions. When you learn to let go and allow others to help, you'll find that your feelings of being overwhelmed will subside and you'll be able to focus on the things that make your life fulfilling and successful.

## System #4: The Systems Solution Selector

When I first started traveling as a speaker and author, all too often I'd open my suitcase to find that I'd forgotten my aftershave, toothpaste, or some other toiletry item. I'd end up in the hotel gift shop, having to spend time and money to replace the items I'd forgotten. Then I created a packing checklist. Every time I get ready to leave for a trip, I pull out my list, put each item in my suitcase, and bingo! No more missing items when I arrive at the hotel.

My packing checklist is an example of a *system* that helps me stay out of being overwhelmed. Systems allow you to automate the tasks that are still on your 80 Percent List so you don't have to think about them anymore. Systems group tasks together into categories, so you see them as one entity instead of a bunch of items on a long to-do list. Systems simplify your life and let you concentrate on the things that will mean the most and produce the greatest result. Systems are practical ways that lead you out of feeling overwhelmed and into success.

As a financial planner, the first thing I do with clients is to help them systematize their finances. We set up monthly contributions to their IRAs and 401(k)s that are deducted automatically from their paychecks or checking accounts. I encourage them to take advantage of tools such as automatic bill pay for their credit cards, utilities, mortgage loans, and so on. We schedule regular check-in phone calls throughout the year so neither of us has to take the time to schedule calls individually. To a person, my clients thank me for helping them take an area of their lives that can seem overwhelming and making it much easier to manage.

Use the following short brainstorming exercise to create systems to help you streamline your life and write your ideas on the form on page 91.

1. Identify a challenge you're facing or an area where you're feeling overwhelmed. (You also can choose a goal that is part of your 20 Percent List.) Write the challenge/area/goal at the top of the form.

2. Under it, write three possible systems that can help you face the challenge, eliminate overwhelm, or pursue the goal. For example, you have too many projects at work and you're not able to focus enough time on any of them. The goal is to manage all your projects effectively. Potential systems would include (a) "block time," where you focus on one project for two hours and don't allow distractions; (b) project management software that will help you track how each project is progressing; (c) leveraging or delegating certain parts of the projects so you can be working on one while progress is being made on another; (d) scheduling regular meetings or e-mail updates with co-workers and your boss to track progress and spot potential challenges before they get too big; and so on. Come up with at least three systems that will alleviate your challenge or help you with your goal.

**3.** Choose one system and implement it immediately. If it works, implement another. If there are still challenges, come up with other systems that will help you.

Here are some examples of simple systems that will make your life easier and help you stay out of being overwhelmed:

⇒ Designate specific times during your workday to answer e-mails or return phone calls. One of my clients, an attorney, hated playing "phone tag" with clients and being interrupted by calls when he was in meetings. The attorney established a system where he would return calls at the same time each day. Clients were told he would call them back between 1 and 2 p.m. either that day or the next. The attorney was happy because he could get his work done, and his clients felt that their calls were being returned in a timely manner.

⇒ Automate any repetitive task. Do you have trouble keeping track of your keys or other personal items? Put them in the same place whenever you come in. Use automatic bill pay for a recurring expense that doesn't change, like the cable bill. One area you *must* automate is saving for retirement. The only way most of us will put aside money for retirement or emergencies is if we don't have to think about socking it away. Utilize all of the computerized tools and systems available to you to ensure that money is going toward your retirement and savings.

⇒ Use checklists. If you have trouble getting the kids to school on time in the morning, post a checklist on the wall and

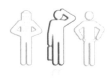

# Systems Solution Selector™

Challenge/Area/Goal:

## List 3 Practical Systems

1

2

3

"To Make Something Powerful,
You Need to Make It Practical"

encourage them to mark off each task when they accomplish it. Hands and face washed? Check. Bed made? Check. Dressed? Check. Breakfast? Check. Teeth brushed? Check. How much easier would it be for you to get your kids out of the door in time for school if they followed a basic routine?

⇒ Look at your work with the idea of systematizing any repetitive tasks. Maybe it's setting aside one hour each week to go over your accounts payable and receivable. Maybe it's entering notes in your BlackBerry as soon as you leave a meeting. Maybe it's utilizing your computer or phone system to send you reminder messages for important events or deadlines. The less thought, time, and energy you have to devote to repetitive tasks, the more resources you will have to focus on the things that really matter.

You probably can identify several scenarios that would save you time and frustration if you create a system to handle them. Systems allow you to focus on what you love to do and what you're great at doing. As a result, you're more likely to feel more fulfilled and get better results.

Systems also can help you prevent one of the greatest dream killers and creators of feeling overwhelmed in our lives: procrastination. When you're overwhelmed, it's easy to put off the tasks that you don't want to do anyway so you can handle the "urgent" stuff that's in front of you. But putting things off almost always makes you feel more overwhelmed, not less. And putting certain things off can be detrimental to your health, happiness, and success. If you put off working on your finances, taking care of your health, or spending time with your spouse, those areas will only get worse due to your neglect, and you're guaranteed to feel a lot more overwhelmed at the end of the road.

Luckily, systems can help you control procrastination, simply because systems make things automatic. If you create a system for scheduling medical appointments, you're more likely to keep them. Set up automatic payments on your credit cards and you'll be less likely to fall behind on your bills. You even can create systems for nurturing your relationship, such as a daily call from work, or a weekly date night no matter what. Human beings are creatures of routine, and you can use this tendency to help you take care of what is truly important. I always say, "To make something powerful you need to make it practical." Very few people can rely completely on self-discipline to attain their goals. Systems allow you to put the journey of your life on "cruise control." I don't know of a better way out of being overwhelmed and moving into success than the implementation of simple, practical systems.

## System #5: The Future Response Formula

The final key to banishing being overwhelmed from your life is to *plan in advance how you will deal with life circumstances.* Even with the best systems and the optimum dream team, it's not likely that you will eliminate completely the events that cause you to feel overwhelmed. We all will be faced with times when the kids get sick, the toilet backs up, taxes are due, a last-minute work project gets dumped on our desks, and so on. Situations that are overwhelming are a fact of life. However, how you deal with those situations can make the difference between spending thirty seconds in being overwhelmed or making feeling overwhelmed a way of life.

When we're faced with a problem or something unexpected, what do we usually do? We react without even thinking about it. If you've ever come close to having a car accident, you know what reaction can be like: without thinking, you swerve to avoid the collision. In times of danger, reaction can be a very good thing. However, when it comes to most things, knee-jerk reactions get you into trouble. Your kids do something wrong and you yell at them. Your spouse snaps at you and you snap back. The stock market drops and you panic. You hear a rumor of layoffs at work and immediately call the boss wanting to know if you need to look for another job. Instead of reacting automatically to events, you need to *respond.* This entails taking control of your emotions and using your brain to figure out the best way to handle situations that come up. You need to learn to use the Future Response Formula that I learned from Jack Canfield, coauthor of the *Chicken Soup for the Soul* series. It looks like this:

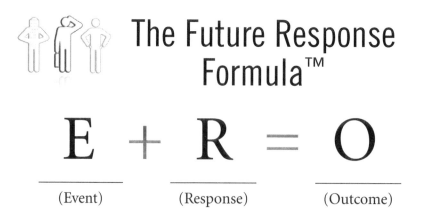

## The Future Response Formula™

$$E + R = O$$

(Event)  (Response)  (Outcome)

### "Change Your Focus"

We have little to no control over most of the events in our lives. However, we do control our thoughts, attitudes, choices, and decisions—our *response* to those events. When we are in control of our responses, we are more likely to be able to affect the outcome of the situation. And that can make a world of difference in how overwhelmed we feel.

The best way to use this formula effectively is to *always keep your outcome in mind no matter what the circumstances.* Let me give you an example that I see all the time. A client called and said, "The stock market just dropped two hundred points. I want you to sell all my stocks and put the money into CDs. That's the only way I can keep my money safe." The event was a two-hundred-point drop in the market. But my client wasn't responding—he was reacting due to his fear of losing money. He'd forgotten his outcome, and as a result, he could have made a very big mistake.

My job as his adviser was to refocus him on his ultimate goal. I replied, "Tom, remember that your outcome was a comfortable retirement. If you check your overall portfolio, you'll see that you're still on track to be ready to retire in ten years or less. Also, that two-hundred-point drop is only for the Dow Jones. The rest of the market is holding steady, and some of your stocks are actually up. How do you want to respond to this situation?" Tom agreed to check his portfolio again, and, as long as he could see he would be able to retire in ten or so years, he would leave things as they are.

Not long ago I used this formula for clients who were having problems with their eleven-year-old son, Scott. The couple was getting a divorce, and they sent their son to therapy for his behavioral issues. Even though I'm a financial advisor, not a therapist, I wanted to help the boy, so I asked the parents if I could talk with Scott privately. I sat the boy down and asked, "I hear you're having some problems. What's going on?"

"My parents are getting divorced," he said.

"That's terrible," I said. Then I explained the Future Response Formula. "The event in your life is your parents' divorce," I said. "How have you been reacting to that?"

"I'm angry. I hate that my parents say bad things about each other. I'm getting bad grades and having fights at school," he told me.

"Is that the way you want things to be?" He shook his head. "You know, you can't control events, but you can control how you respond to them," I continued. "If you could have a good outcome and make the best of this situation, how would you respond?"

> If you keep your focus on your outcome, step back from your emotional reaction to events, and allow yourself to respond to them instead, then you're more likely to not be overwhelmed and make better decisions for your life.

He thought for a minute. "I'd talk to my parents and ask them not to say bad things about each other. Also, one of the reasons my grades are down is that I'm spending three nights a week at my dad's apartment, and I always forget stuff for my homework. I'd rather stay at Mom's house during the week and go to Dad's on weekends."

"That sounds like a great response," I told him. We went back to his parents, and I explained to them how Scott would like to respond to their situation. Two months later the parents called me and said, "Louis, that formula you taught our son helped him more than four months of therapy!"

Far too many people react rather than respond to events in the stock market, at home, or on the job, and make decisions that cost them dearly in the long run. If you keep your focus on your outcome, step back from your emotional reaction to events, and allow yourself to respond to them instead, then you're more likely to not be overwhelmed and make better decisions for your life.

Once you understand the power of the response formula, you can use it to prepare yourself for situations that might otherwise cause you to feel overwhelmed. You literally can plan your response to future events. If you have a particular situation in which you know you regularly react or experience feeling overwhelmed, try using the Future Response Formula *before* you find yourself in the middle of things. Maybe you react with frustration and are overwhelmed if your daycare arrangements fall through, or your child gets sick and you have to leave work. What could you do to ensure that you respond to those circumstances rather than react? The easiest way is to set up systems and backup systems to help you handle these events. Maybe you have an emergency babysitter. Maybe you set up an arrangement with a relative who can take care of your child until you arrive. Maybe you and a co-worker agree to cover for each other in case of family emergencies. Maybe you talk to your boss about being able to work from home should you have to care for your child. Simply having thought through situations that cause you stress and creating solutions for them in advance will keep you out of being overwhelmed and help you feel more relaxed and in control.

*Responsibility is the ability to respond rather than react.* Being responsible means that you are making a conscious choice to behave in a way that will move you closer to your ideal outcome. Winston Churchill once said, "The price of greatness is responsibility." You must decide if you're willing to direct your thoughts and emotions, to respond to events rather than react to them, to focus on your ideal outcomes, and to make sure your choices are leading you toward those outcomes. Developing and using systems, building your dream team, setting your boundaries, and responding rather than reacting will allow you to approach the circumstances of your life more relaxed and more in control.

There's a story about an Elizabethan mansion in England that had a maze in its garden. Every year visitors would come from all over the world to enjoy getting lost in the maze's twists and turns. It would take an average time of an hour for anyone to walk the maze from one end to the other—unless you knew the secret. If you turned right at every junction, you could complete the maze in less than five minutes. In the same way, you can leave the maze of overwhelm by knowing the secrets of simplification—including the 80/20 List, boundary setting and saying no effectively, building your dream team of support, creating systems to streamline your life, and anticipating challenges so you can respond rather than react. These are the "right" turns that will help you stay relaxed and in control as you navigate the maze of life.

Overworked, Overwhelmed, and Underpaid

*underpaid*

# CHAPTER FOUR

# From Underpaid to Doing Well Through Meaningful Work

In this chapter, you'll discover . . .

⇒ the five reasons you may feel underpaid;

⇒ the key to greater compensation is to increase the value you give and receive (you can do this by focusing on your strengths and using them to create greater profit for you and your business);

⇒ how to create a business plan for "You, Inc." (your work), including a vision, specific goals and outcomes, and a balance sheet of assets and liabilities;

⇒ ways to enhance your strengths through investments of time, money, and resources;

⇒ secrets for mitigating, delegating, or eliminating weaknesses; and

⇒ how to spot and evaluate opportunities to accelerate your income.

"Louis, I drag myself home from work every night and feel I haven't accomplished anything, and I don't like what I'm doing anyway. I walk through the door and collapse into a chair, exhausted. I don't get paid enough to work like that . . ."

"Every month I find myself sitting at my desk trying to figure out how I'll pay the bills. Every month it seems I end up with less money than I need. I've asked my boss for a raise but she says things are tight. She offered me a better title but no more money. The job market's terrible so I don't want to quit, but I don't get paid enough to provide the lifestyle my family deserves . . . What'll I do?"

"Louis, I enjoy work, but lately I'm spending a lot more time on the job and it's taking away from my family life. Just this week I got back late from yet another business trip, and there was a note on the refrigerator about a meeting with my daughter's teacher. My little girl is having problems at school and I didn't even realize it! I don't get paid enough to be away from my family like this . . ."

I hear stories like these all the time, from people in my office, from attendees at my seminars, and from other professionals I encounter across the United States. Most of us feel under-compensated and undervalued. If you, too, are feeling underpaid, it's not surprising, since wage growth has been stagnant for most workers for more than thirty years. According to the Economic Policy Institute, between 1979 and 2006 productivity increased over 67 percent, and the amount of time spent on the job has increased by a full eight weeks per year for each worker. Yet median worker salaries went up by *less than 9 per-cent*—an average increase of 0.3 percent per year. For the 2004 median household income of $54,061, that would have meant a raise of just $1,622. And with inflation averaging 2.69 percent per year over the same seven-year period, it's clear that even the best-paid workers aren't keeping up with inflation. Indeed, between 2000 and 2004, median family income in the United States fell by 3 percent.

In 2005/2006, Salary.com did an online job satisfaction survey of almost fourteen thousand workers and four hundred human resources managers. Sixty-five percent of respondents planned on looking for a new job in the next three months, and the majority cited inadequate compensation as the main reason. When Salary.com analyzed the salaries of these employees, they found that, according to job benchmarks, around 20 percent were underpaid, and approximately 30 percent were paid so far below market average that it is likely they were given a title in lieu of a raise at some point. That means half of us are either underpaid or paid less than our job titles indicate. However, feeling underpaid doesn't have to be tied to a certain level of compensation. It also can be caused by disliking what our work requires. For example, many of my clients make a six-figure income, but they're unhappy with the time they have to spend away from their family.

As with overwork and overwhelm, underpaid is primarily a feeling based on components that are practical and emotional. I believe that feeling underpaid arises from one (or more) of five reasons.

## Reason #1: You really *are* paid less than you're worth.

You're a part of the 50 percent whose compensation is below industry standards or below your current job title. Maybe you were a bad negotiator when you were hired, or you didn't research comparable salaries in your industry. Maybe you started in a lower-paying job and your subsequent salary has been based on that amount. Maybe when you asked for a raise, you were offered a new title without any more money. Now you're a "Supervisor" or "Director" or "Department Head," but you're not paid the same as other supervisors because you're not doing the same job.

If you are truly underpaid, you need knowledge and action. First, you must educate yourself on appropriate compensation for your job in your industry. Go to Web sites like Salary.com and Monster.com to check current pay levels for jobs like yours. You'll need to compare your job responsibilities with people who have the same title in other firms to see if you are "over-titled" for the job you do.

Second, you must take action. You need to learn to "blow your own horn" to ensure your efforts are acknowledged and compensated. Before your next performance review, document all the value you are providing and the tasks you have taken on. Your documentation should include tangible accomplishments like the amount of money you have saved or made the company, or increases to efficiency and results. Compare what you actually do on the job to your job description, and show how you are exceeding the requirements in significant ways. Give the documentation to your supervisor and/or HR department in advance of your review, along with your proposal for a raise, a promotion, comp time, and so on.

At your performance review, be prepared to make your case clearly and positively, and know what your bottom line would be. Is the raise or promotion or comp time an absolute must for you? If so, how much of a raise? What promotion? If your needs are not met, what will your fallback position be? Remember, as a last resort you can always leave the job. The main thing is not to be one of the majority of workers who feel underpaid and/or under-acknowledged and do nothing about it except complain. That's a recipe for frustration and stress.

## Reason #2: You don't make enough to support the lifestyle you desire (or worse, the lifestyle you already have).

Do you know the definition of a rich man? One whose income exceeds expenses by 10 percent. And the definition of a poor man? One whose expenses exceed income by 10 percent. Some people feel underpaid because they don't have enough money to cover their lifestyle. Others have enough for their current needs but envy their neighbors' big-screen TV and new car. If you don't have enough money to cover your expenses, you must get into the habit of living within your means. Otherwise, even when you increase your income, you will tend to continue to spend more than you make. Spending less than you earn is the only way you can build a future for yourself and your family. It's also the most direct way to increase your income immediately—cutting your expenses by 5 percent is the equivalent of giving yourself a 5 percent raise. If at the end of the month you look at your income and see a surplus after all your bills are paid, you will feel much wealthier and happier.

> Spending less than you earn is the only way you can build a future for yourself and your family.

One of the simplest ways to start spending less than you earn is to pay yourself first—that is, put aside a certain percentage of your income to invest in savings, an emergency contingency account, retirement accounts, and so on. If you go to my Web site, www.louisbarajas.com, you'll find a bonus chapter that discusses clear and simple ways you can build a financial plan for yourself and your family.

### Reason #3: You're putting in more effort at work than you're being compensated for.

If you work a lot of overtime but receive neither extra pay nor time off to compensate, you can feel underpaid. Even if you don't work much overtime, you may feel you're providing a lot of unrecognized and uncompensated value on the job. Perhaps you're an administrative assistant who's doing a lot of the work of your manager. Perhaps your extra efforts make your boss look really good, but you get very little recognition for it. Perhaps you take on additional responsibilities that aren't part of your job description. Maybe you end up being the "numbers cruncher" for your team because numbers are your strong suit, even though your official role is salesperson. Or you're a teacher at school and you've taken on running an after-school clinic for kids who aren't reading to grade level.

If you're working overtime for no compensation, you will need to either change jobs, change expectations, or change the way you work. First, do a reality check. Are you really doing more than others in the same kind of job? Are other people doing the same work and are more efficient than you? You may be better off asking for additional help rather than more money. Is the extra work you are doing valued by the company or organization? That after-school program might be absolutely necessary in your eyes, but if your school district doesn't fund such programs, you will be hard-pressed to make a case for more compensation for creating one.

Overworked, Overwhelmed, and Underpaid

You also must be familiar with your company's policies. If your company does not allow for paid time off to compensate for overtime, asking for comp time will not fly. You'd be better off negotiating for some other benefit, like telecommuting one day a week, or asking for technical support or additional personnel so you can get the work done in less time. You may need to say no to requests for extra work that isn't compensated and to negotiate compensation for the areas where you are asked to do more than others.

## Reason #4: Work is taking you away from what's really important to you.

Sometimes the feeling of being underpaid is linked to resentment that your work prevents you from the activities or people that matter even more. If you find yourself saying things like, "I don't get paid enough to be on the road all the time," or "This job isn't worth being away from my family so much," or "There isn't enough money in the world to compensate for not watching my kids grow up," then you've found the reason behind your feelings. Look at the life blueprint you created in chapter 2, and see if there is a mismatch between the amount of time and focus you devote to your job and the amount you want to devote to other areas, values, relationships, and roles. In chapter 5 we'll discuss fitting your work into your life rather than the other way around.

## Reason #5: You don't enjoy your work.

One of the biggest differences between feeling adequately compensated and underpaid isn't money, but a feeling of doing something that you do well and enjoy. If you've ever done volunteer work that you loved but weren't paid for, or you worked round the clock on a project simply because you loved what you were doing, then you understand that compensation doesn't have to be monetary. In fact, people usu-

**Job satisfaction trumps compensation almost every time.**

ally experience the greatest satisfaction when they like their work, they're good at what they do, and they feel they're being rewarded fairly. On the other hand, people who don't like their work and don't feel their talents and abilities are being used to their fullest are more likely to look for another job even if they're offered higher pay. Job satisfaction trumps compensation almost every time. And one of the most important factors of job satisfaction is the feeling that we have the opportunity to use our talents and abilities. Much of the rest of this chapter will help you define what you love to do and what you have the potential to excel at doing. Then you'll learn how to use your talents and abilities to create work that will be well compensated and enjoyable.

## The Solution to Feeling Underpaid

Most people feel underpaid when there is a disconnect between the value they provide and the value they receive as a result of that work. If you aren't paid adequately, you're not receiving enough monetary value. If you don't feel appreciated or you don't enjoy what you do, you're not receiving enough emotional value. If you put in a lot of uncompensated time or your work takes you away from other aspects of your life, you feel that the exchange of value is uneven. You must shift your focus toward what you can do to *increase the value you give and receive* rather than simply asking to get more from your job. When you increase either the monetary or emotional value you receive from work, you will find that you feel more appropriately compensated. And when you increase the value you give—and other people agree that you are providing more value—then you are likely to increase your income as well.

You can maximize your value by *focusing on your strengths*. Strengths are shorthand for, "Do more of what you do well, do it more frequently, and do it in ways that create profit for you and your business." You're hired for a job because someone believes you will create value for the money you will be paid. Doesn't it make sense that you would be able to create more value with your strengths? Don't you enjoy your work more when you do a great job, and aren't you more likely to do a great job when you're using your talents and strengths? When you focus on your strengths, you will find it easier to do well and your work will be more meaningful.

> One of the most important factors of job satisfaction is the feeling that we have the opportunity to use our talents and abilities.

The strategies for eliminating feeling underpaid from your life fall into two categories: *passion* and *potential*. Passion is what drives us all, but long ago most of us ceased feeling excited about what we do. A lot of people treat their jobs the same way they treat their long-term relationships: as an obligation rather than a joy. When we put as little passion as possible into our jobs, is it any wonder that we get very little in return? I believe that your job should be something you love to do—what I call an "occu-passion." People who have passion about work aren't interested in retirement because they love what they do and would do it forever. The secret is to discover your passion and then link it to your work. Then you will value your work more highly, and others will as well.

The second category of strategy is *potential*. No matter how much you give to your work, it represents a mere fraction of your true potential. To earn more, you need to learn to use more of your potential, either on the job or in other opportunities. But you also need to be smart. Remember the 80/20 principle: 20 percent of our efforts produce 80 percent of our results. Your 20 percent is composed of the unique combination of talents, abilities, knowledge, and skills that make you shine. You are most effective, produce the best results, and enjoy yourself the most when you can apply your strengths at work. Knowing and utilizing your strengths allows you to tap into more of your potential year after year. It also opens your mind to new possibilities for creating more income. When you combine passion and potential, work starts feeling more like a calling. It also is more fun and rewarding, both financially and emotionally.

> The secret is to discover your passion and then link it to your work. Then you will value your work more highly, and others will as well.

## You, Inc.

Imagine you are walking into the headquarters of a multimillion-dollar corporation. The reception area is opulent yet tasteful; the atmosphere is one of focused activity and purposeful achievement. This is obviously a place where important things are accomplished effectively and with excellence. You look up on the wall behind the reception desk—and you see the words "YOU, INC." with your name listed as "Founder, President, and CEO"!

The average person will have seven different careers in his or her work lifetimes—*careers*, not jobs. To make sure you are adequately compensated at each step along the way, you must view your work as if it were a business that you are responsible for guiding to optimum enjoyment, productivity, and profitability. You need to plan your business life as carefully as a CEO or president of a company plans the life of the business. *You are the founder, president, and CEO of the "company" of You, Inc.* Whether you are an employee, a boss, or an entrepreneur, you need to treat your professional life as if you are in charge of the success or failure of your business—because you are. Only you can provide the passion and potential that will increase the results of You, Inc., and thus increase your income.

There are three systems that will help you increase your passion and use more of your potential. The Business Plan for You, Inc., will help you change your mind-set by creating a vision and plan for your work life that will make your passion practical. The Talent Identifier and Strengths Builder will allow you to identify your unique abilities and help you eliminate or mitigate areas of your work life where you are not strong. Finally, the Income Opportunity Accelerator will show you how to use what you are already great at to earn more income, either as part of your current job or in addition to it.

> The average person will have seven different careers in his or her work lifetimes—*careers*, not jobs.

### ◇ System #1: The Business Plan for You, Inc.

Every business starts with a vision that includes its identity; what it does; who its customer is; its income goals for each month, year, five years, and decade; and how it plans to grow within its particular niche. A business plan also includes a list of the assets the business holds and the liabilities it must handle in order to make a profit. The business plan for You, Inc., must contain the same elements. You must have a *vision* of your business life: you must know who you are in your business, what you do, and whom your work life serves. Your vision must inspire and excite you so you will be willing to put in the work to make it happen. Your business plan must have *specific goals and outcomes*, not just for the amount of money you wish to make but also for the value you wish to provide. Finally, you must assess where you are starting from—your current *"balance sheet"* of assets and liabilities, whether they include tangible elements like money or education, or more intangible ones like beliefs, habits, skills, and identity.

**Step 1: The Vision for You, Inc.** Jim Collins, author of *Good to Great: Why Some Companies Make the Leap . . . and Others Don't,* says that companies move from good to great when they focus their efforts on three factors: (1) doing what they love to do, (2) doing what they're great at, and (3) doing what makes a profit. These three factors apply equally to the vision you must create for your work life. No matter how much money a career has the potential to make, unless you love what you do, you're not likely to make a go of it. On the other hand, when you find a job that is tied to something that you'd do even if nobody paid you to do it, then you've found work that will get you up in the morning and keep you going for the long haul.

Creating a vision for your work can help you decide what career to start. If you already have a career, it can help you figure out how to make it more enjoyable, or help you make the decision to do something else. When your vision for your work matches the reality of what you're doing, you have a recipe for success and fulfillment. Here are your steps for creating your work vision. This exercise should take about thirty minutes to an hour.

1. Write a description of everything you love to do at your current job. Do you like talking with people? Making connections? Persuading? Pulling together a team and orchestrating their efforts? Helping people? Researching a problem? Think about other jobs you have held. What did you enjoy about them? Write every aspect of your current or past employment that you have truly enjoyed.

2. Next, write down everything you enjoy doing outside of work, including hobbies, volunteer work, recreation, and so on. What specifically do you enjoy about these endeavors? You may find some common elements between this list and the first one. If you like teambuilding at work, you may coach Little League on weekends. If you like crossword puzzles, you may find that your ideal job involves some kind of problem solving. Circle any elements the two lists have in common.

3. Based on your lists, how many different kinds of occupations/ businesses could you participate in and enjoy? Someone who enjoys numbers could be an analyst, accountant, teacher, researcher, statistician, bookkeeper, financial advisor, and so on. Someone who enjoys leading others could be a coach, supervisor, executive, speaker/ presenter, trainer, consultant, and more. Write down every possible job or business that would allow you to make money doing what you enjoy.

**4.** Now, create a vision for your ideal job. This can be a version of your current occupation at its best, or something completely different. What would you do if you could choose any job in the world? Imagine going to work at a job that excites you, where time seems to fly by because you are so engrossed. Write a detailed description of your day at work. How do you spend your time? Do you work mostly by yourself, or with a team? How do you interact with others? Does your work involve travel, or do you work from home part of the time? Do you receive a lot of recognition, or is doing a great job enough to make you happy? How do you feel when you finish work each day?

You have just described your occu-passion, the job you would do even if you weren't paid to do it. The truth is, you are more likely to be paid well for doing what you love because you will put in more of your time, energy, and focus, and you will be better at it as a result. Like the title of the self-help classic says, do what you love and the money will follow.

**Step 2: The Goals for You, Inc.** Now that you have your vision for your occu-passion, you can start devising a plan to make it real. You may have heard, "Seeing is believing," but actually vision and passion precede believing, and believing precedes reality. Indeed, changing your vision is the only way reality ever changes. And when you are passionate about your vision, you will have the drive and energy to make it real.

Your plan begins with specific professional and financial goals for the business of You, Inc. Professional goals deal with the results of

# Your Work Vision™

Write a Description of Everthing You Love to Do at Your Current Job

1

Write Down Everything You Enjoy Doing Outside of Work

2

Based on Above, How Many Different Kinds of Occupation/Businesses Could You Participate In & Enjoy

3

Create a Vision for Your Ideal Job

4

your work life, and financial goals address the amount of money you will earn.

*1. Professional Goals:* Look at the description of your ideal job/ career. If you were creating a one-year plan for this business, what would it include? What are your top one-year goals for yourself in your job/career? (If your ideal job is not the one you're currently in, your first goal might be to devise a plan for leaving your present job.) Assume you're looking back on your life one year from now. What will you need to have done to feel successful and fulfilled?

Next to each goal, write why it is important for you to accomplish it. To feel as though you are living your purpose? To learn and grow? To make a difference? To take care of your family? To improve your industry? To stand out as an example of excellence in your field? To care for the people in your business? A powerful "why" is the energy that will help you attain your goals in the face of any obstacles and challenges.

Now extend your "business plan" into the future. What are your goals for the next five years? The next ten? If you were getting ready to retire, what would you want to have accomplished between now and then?

*2. Financial Goals:* Write down your annual income for the past year. Next to it, write down the amount you would like to earn this year from the job you described in your vision. Make sure the new number is at least 10 percent larger than last year's income. (If you feel that you could increase your income by a greater percentage, write that number down.) How would you feel if you were earning that amount by doing work you enjoy?

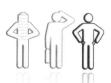

# The Goals for You, Inc.™

## Professional Goals

Idea Job/Career:

| One-Year Goals | Why Is It Important? |
|---|---|
| 1 | |
| 2 | |
| 3 | |
| 4 | |
| 5 | |

| Five and Ten-Year Goals | Why Is It Important? |
|---|---|
| 1 | |
| 2 | |
| 3 | |
| 4 | |
| 5 | |

Underneath this new income figure, write how much you want to make each year for the next ten years. Increase each yearly number by a minimum of 10 percent. (By the way, with a yearly increase of just 10 percent you will double your income in less than eight years!)

Under the list of your financial goals, write all your reasons for making these goals a reality. Why do you want to make more money? So you'll feel well paid at last? So your family can have a better lifestyle? So you can retire sooner, send your kids to college, or give more to a cause or organization? Will earning more give you confidence? Will it allow you to take advantage of career opportunities? Will it help you sleep better? Will there be less stress in your marriage? Don't worry about *how* you will increase your income. Remember, vision and passion must precede creation, and passion and vision come from your personal reasons for attaining your goals.

**Step 3: The Balance Sheet for You, Inc.** Every business needs an accurate balance sheet that enumerates its assets and liabilities. Your personal balance sheet is just as vital to the business of You, Inc. You need to know the assets you can use to make your work life a success, and you must acknowledge the liabilities that must be reduced, eliminated, or dealt with so you can pursue the well-compensated, meaningful work of your occu-passion.

*1. Assets:* On the Balance Sheet for You, Inc. form on page 121, in the first column, "Experience," list the skills, knowledge, habits, and experience you already possess that could help you in your career. Professional degrees, classes, and time spent in the same kind of work all go in this

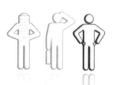

# The Goals for You, Inc.™

## Financial Goals

Idea Job/Career:

| Annual Income for the Past Year | Income You Would Like to Earn this Year | |
|---|---|---|
| | | |
| **How Would You Feel If You Were Earning That Amount?** | **Income for the Next Ten Years** | |
| | 1 | |
| | 2 | |
| | 3 | |
| | 4 | |
| | 5 | |
| | 1 | |
| | 2 | |
| | 3 | |
| | 4 | |
| | 5 | |

### Reasons Why These Goals Should Be Plenty

1
2
3
4
5

column. Why will you be great at this ideal job of yours? Be specific. The more detail you provide, the better.

In the second column, "Mental Resources," list all the beliefs you have about why you can succeed in your ideal career. What do you believe you are capable of? Where have you been successful before? Why are you suited for this job? Why are you committed to making this happen? What character traits do you possess that will help you succeed? Imagine you had to sell yourself to someone who was hiring you. What would you say that would make it obvious you are the best person for this job/career/business?

In the third column, "Physical Resources," list any tangible assets that you can apply to your ideal job. This includes financial resources like savings or liquid assets; equipment like computers, laptops, cell phones, PDAs, automobiles, and tools; services like Internet connections, phone service, and professional memberships; space to run the business (a room in your house, if appropriate); and so on. Make sure you include resources you have access to but don't necessarily own. Do you have access to lines of credit? Equity in your home? Possible investors or business partners? List every resource you either own or have access to.

*2. Liabilities:* On another sheet, note any liabilities in terms of your experience, mental resources, and physical resources. What experience are you currently missing that you will need? What knowledge, skills, or habits must you develop? Are there any habits that you must eliminate for you to be successful? If you want to become a manager, for example, and you're disorganized, you will need to eliminate messiness and develop better organizational skills.

Overworked, Overwhelmed, and Underpaid

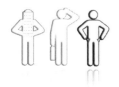

# Balance Sheet
# for You, Inc.™

| | Experience | Mental Resources | Physical Resources |
|---|---|---|---|
| 1 | | | |
| 2 | | | |
| 3 | | | |
| 4 | | | |
| 5 | | | |
| 6 | | | |
| 7 | | | |

In terms of your physical resources, what are your current liabilities? What would you need in your ideal job that you currently do not possess or have access to? Say you wanted to start your own business and needed ten thousand dollars in seed money. However, you have no equity in your home, a lot of credit card debt, and no one to invest in your business. Those would be considered liabilities. Or perhaps you wanted to run a home-based business, but currently you have no space to do so other than your kitchen table. Lack of space would be a liability.

Finally, look at your mental resources. What beliefs do you have about yourself that might get in the way of your ideal job? What beliefs do you have about business, about money, about effort and reward, about the sacrifices your ideal job might require? What doubts do you have about yourself and your abilities? How do you see yourself? Many of us are blind to our own inner treasures. We can't see our resources of strength, focus, creativity, discipline, and diligence, because we have been trained from the cradle to believe that's not who we are. How do you see yourself when it comes to your ability to create your ideal career? Do you lack support from the people around you? (An unsupportive spouse or life partner is one of the biggest obstacles to success.) Capture all the reasons why you can't possibly succeed. It's better to get them all out on paper now instead of letting them fester unexpressed and having them sabotage your efforts later on.

*3. Turn your liabilities around.* Look at the items on your list of liabilities and ask, "How can I either eliminate or mitigate these?" In the "Experience" column, can you get additional training? Acquire more knowledge? Develop new skills? Eliminate old habits and replace them with new ones? Take the three liabilities that you feel are the most pressing and come up with a plan to eliminate or mitigate them in the next ninety days.

In the "Physical Resources" area, how can you gain access to more resources or decrease the impact of these liabilities? If you're carrying a lot of consumer debt, stop spending and start paying off your credit cards. If you don't have access to financial resources, perhaps you can develop a relationship now with the loan officer at a local bank so the resources may be available at a later date. You also could start exploring avenues for gaining investors. If you lack resources like space, material, equipment, and so on, how can you find or acquire what you will need? Include two of the items on your list as part of your ninety-day plan.

You would think that handling the liabilities in the "Mental Resources" area would be the easiest of the three, but often they can prove the most difficult. You must stop focusing on your liabilities and learn to focus on all that you have to offer. Next to each of the items on your mental liabilities list, write the opposite belief. "I never succeed" becomes "I always succeed." "I'm undisciplined" becomes "I'm focused and on task." "Business is too complicated for me" becomes "Business is easy to understand." These alternative beliefs are potential assets that will help the business of You, Inc., to be successful. At the bottom of the column, put the words "If all these are true, then . . ." and then write what your life and business would be like if you believed these alternatives. If you believed you always succeed, how would you act? What would you attempt? How well would you do? If business were easy to understand, what impact would that have on your ideal job? If you were focused and on task, how much easier would your work life be? Every day for the next ninety days, read your list of alternative mental resources and your description of your life and business, and then act as if they were true.

In every business, success comes from maximizing assets while minimizing or eliminating liabilities. To succeed in the business of You, Inc., you must do the same. Once you have done so, you are ready to move ahead to the system that will help you accelerate your earnings and satisfaction exponentially.

## ◇ System #2: The Talent Identifier and Strengths Builder

For the past ten years the Gallup Organization has been amassing data on job satisfaction and what they call "employee engagement"—how positive and productive people are at work. Gallup surveyed more than ten million people worldwide, and discovered only one-third of them strongly agreed with the statement "At work, I have an opportunity to do what I do best every day." Gallup also discovered that people who get a chance to do what they do best are six times more likely to be engaged with their work. Your ultimate assets are not just experience, mental resources, and physical resources, but the resources of your talents and strengths. When your work allows you to utilize your talents and strengths, you are more likely to do well at work and to be well compensated rather than underpaid. You must do your best to optimize the unique talents you bring to the job so you will enjoy your work at a higher level.

Remember the formula for great companies as I described on page 112? First, they *do what they enjoy doing*. You learned how to identify what you enjoy as you created the vision for your ideal job. Second, they *do what they are great at doing*. They focus on jobs and market niches where they can utilize their strengths. Great companies don't try to be all things to all people. If they do, they risk diluting their message and losing market share. Starbucks Coffee learned that lesson when it tried to offer hot breakfast sandwiches and other items that fell outside its initial focus of coffee and other beverages. Its market share suffered, and its earnings were flat. Starbucks' CEO Howard Schultz declared, "We are going back to what we do best—delivering the best coffee in the world served by the most knowledgeable employees." You, too, must focus on developing your strengths and let them guide where and how you devote your energy.

You also need to identify your weaknesses: the things you're naturally not good at doing. *No one* is strong in everything. It's better to spend time and energy developing your strengths than to try to get good at something at which you are weak. If you're not strong in finances, for example, you can study accounting, but you probably won't enjoy it and won't be good at it either. It's better to be truly strong at certain things than to be average in everything. The world rewards great far more than it rewards good, and trying to be a jack-of-all-trades is the path of mediocrity. Your goal is to focus on developing your strengths while you either eliminate or mitigate the areas where you are weak.

According to Tom Rath (leader of Gallup's workplace research and leadership consulting and author of *StrengthsFinder 2.0*), *talent* (a natural way of thinking, feeling, or behaving) multiplied by *investment* (time spent practicing, developing your skills, and building your knowledge base) equals *strength* (the ability to consistently provide near-perfect performance). And strengths, properly applied, can lead to work that is meaningful and well compensated. To discover your own strengths and talents, you can ask yourself the following questions that I use in my own business. They were designed to help you discover your greatest talents and strengths.

## Step 1: Name Your Talents/Gifts/Strengths

**1.** List five things that you do better than most people you know. They can include actual jobs like bookkeeping, teaching, design, and so on, or skills and abilities, like organizing, leading, caring for people, and so on. What are your top five talents, gifts, and strengths?

**2.** On a scale of 1 to 10 (1 being not at all and 10 being absolutely), how much do you enjoy using each of these talents, gifts, and strengths? You may be great at organizing but hate doing it. You could have a talent for drawing but no passion for it, while you have less ability as a speaker but love being in front of people. You'll go much further utilizing the talent you enjoy rather than the talent you don't care much about. Remember, strength is a combination of talent or ability, plus enjoyment, plus investment. Rate each of the five items on your "enjoyment" scale. Your top two talents, gifts, and strengths are the ones you will focus on enhancing and building.

## Step 2: Enhance Your Talents/Gifts/Strengths

In order to become a strength, any talent, gift, or ability requires an investment on your part. You may be a great designer, but you need training and practice before you can start selling that expertise to others. To turn your innate abilities into strengths, you must be prepared to invest time and possibly money in their development. Use the Performance Tools Identifier form to capture the following information.

# Special Gifts Clarifier™

| List 5 Things That You Feel You Do Better Than Most People |
|---|
| **1** |
| **2** |
| **3** |
| **4** |
| **5** |

| Of the 5 You Listed, Select 1 or 2 That You Feel Is Unique Only To You |
|---|
| **1** |
| **2** |

1. Write down one of the top two talents, gifts, and strengths that you identified earlier. Below it, write at least four ways you can increase your capability with this talent. For example, you may have a gift for speaking to groups. How could you get better at it? You could hire a coach. You could join Toastmasters and give speeches every week. You could offer to speak free of charge to nonprofit groups. You could go to see other speakers and learn from them. You could become an expert in one aspect of speaking at a time—eye contact with your audience, or gestures, or vocal variety. Perhaps you're a manager and you enjoy developing the people in your department. You could take courses in psychology or human resources or team-building. You could study how to use language to coach others more effectively. You could teach others how to build better teams. (Sometimes the best way to get better at something is to share it with others.) You could model other executives in your company. You could get some peer-to-peer coaching from other managers.

   On a scale of 1 to 10 (1 being the least and 10 being the most), rate how much your talent or ability would be enhanced by each of the ways you wrote.

2. Next to each performance enhancer, write the investment it will take to implement. All enhancers require investments of time, money, or both. Taking a class might mean a time investment of one night a week for twelve weeks, and a financial investment of a thousand dollars. Setting up a peer-to-peer coaching group may require a time investment of one morning a month and buying your peers breakfast.

3. Now, write down how long it would take for you to implement this performance enhancer. You may be able to set up lunch with a role

model next week, whereas it might take longer to find an appropriate training to increase your leadership skills.

4. Based on the four factors of (a) effectiveness, (b) time investment, (c) financial investment, and (d) immediacy, choose two enhancers that will increase your talent or ability the most. Make sure that one enhancer is something that you can implement immediately, and another is something that may take longer but has the potential to be greatly effective. Create a plan to take action for each enhancer.

## Step 3: Mitigate, Delegate, or Eliminate Your Weaknesses

Most of us think we have to work on our weaknesses first, because that's where we need the most growth. But as I said earlier, our greatest growth comes from our strengths, not our weaknesses. It goes back to the 80/20 Principle: you want to focus the majority of your efforts on the 20 percent that will produce the greatest results—your strengths—rather than on the weaknesses that will return very little on your investment.

I'm not saying that you can ignore your weaknesses. If you're not good at numbers and your work involves yearly budgets, you still have to get the job done. If you're less than great at writing and you're managing a sales team, you're still going to need to express yourself clearly in memos, e-mails, reports, and so on. No one is going to be great at every aspect of any job or profession. However, instead of spending a great deal of time, effort, and frustration trying to become great at your weaknesses, you can look for ways to handle them elegantly. Your goal is to put 80 percent of your effort into your strengths, and 20 percent toward handling your weaknesses. The following exercise will get you started:

1. Write down seven tasks you don't do well or you hate doing in your professional and personal life. Based on this list, what are your weaknesses? Admit them proudly. We all have them, and owning up to them can be liberating. Write your weaknesses on a separate page.

2. For each weakness, ask, "How can I minimize the impact of this? There are three ways to handle weaknesses. First, you can *mitigate* them by getting just a little bit better. If you're working on budgets, perhaps you could get someone to review them with you so you start to get the hang of them. If you're not good at writing, you could take a class in basic business writing, or get someone to edit your reports after you've written them. The goal isn't to be great at your weaknesses—you only have to be "good enough." (On the other hand, the goal with your strengths is to become great, not good.)

   Second, you can *delegate* the tasks in which you are weak. What is a strength for you will be a weakness for someone else, and vice versa. Find (or hire) people whose strengths complement your weaknesses, and allow them to take on the tasks you hate. Remember, however, delegation does not mean abdication. Ultimately you are responsible for the end results required by your job, whether they fall into your areas of strength or weakness. If you delegate the budgeting function of your job, for example, you must set out the guidelines for whoever takes it on, check the figures and assumptions of the budget, and be willing to approve the final product. I also suggest that, when you delegate, you give credit where credit is due. Let other people shine at what they do best, and you do the same.

   Third, you can figure out ways to *eliminate* tasks that are in your areas of weakness. If numbers aren't your strong suit, can you pass

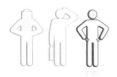

# Performance Tools
# Identifier™

Special Gift:

| List Tools That Will Enhance Your Special Gift | | |
|---|---|---|
| Performance Enhancer | Financial Investment | Time Investment |
| 1 | | |
| 2 | | |
| 3 | | |
| 4 | | |
| Of the 4 You Listed, Select 2 Enhancers That Will Increase Your Talent or Ability the Most. | | |
| 1 | | |
| 2 | | |

the details of budgeting to a colleague while you review the final recommendations? If you hate to write, can you change your sales report from a written document to a weekly call with your boss, followed up with an e-mail that lays out the numbers? Instead of trying to do the job yourself, you can involve a team of people who are able to express their unique gifts in their work, which will give them more fulfillment and will give you a much higher-performing team.

3. Review the seven tasks you hate or don't do well. Which of these can you mitigate, delegate, or eliminate? Come up with creative ways to decrease the effort you are expending on these tasks.

4. Finally, you also need to be willing to let go. Sometimes we hold on to tasks because they are part of what we consider our roles, even though we are really bad at these things. I've known husbands who insist on managing the family finances even when their wives are better with money, or bosses who run sales meetings when they're more comfortable with figures than with people. Remember, greatness doesn't come from being good at everything; it comes from being outstanding in a few things and letting other people be outstanding at others. Be willing to own your strengths and your weaknesses, and let go of the parts of your job or your role in which you will never be more than mediocre.

Think how free you will feel when these tasks are no longer weighing over your head, or how much more you would enjoy your work if you spent 80 percent of your time focused on the things you do well rather than the things you don't! One of the most important components of feeling happy about your work is the opportunity to use your strengths.

## ◇ System #3: The Income Opportunity Accelerator

Even if you're using your strengths and creating outstanding results at a job that has meaning for you, it's still possible that you aren't being compensated at the level you desire and deserve. If this is true, you must *increase your income*. Certainly, asking for a raise or finding a different job that pays more can put more money in your pocket. Cutting your expenses can help too. But here's the real secret for increasing your income, whether you stay at your current job or move to another: *to add more income, you must add more value.*

Say you were earning $25,000 and working 40 hours a week. If you wanted to make $50,000 in the same job, you'd have to work 80 hours; to make $100,000 you'd have to work 160 hours—and there are only 168 hours in the week! But who wants to work 80 or 100 hours a week? Even if it were possible, it's not sustainable. However, are there people who make $50,000 or $100,000 a year and work less than 40 hours a week? Of course. That's because the *value* they provide at work is perceived as worth the higher salary. If you really want to increase your income, you must focus on developing specific ways to provide more value on the job.

Value is both objective and subjective. It is objective in terms of the complexity of your job, the degree of training and/or education that's required, the amount of work done, and so on. An internal medicine doctor's value is very high when compared to a nurse's aide, for example, but it is lower than that of a medical specialist like a surgeon, oncologist, and so on. But value is subjective when it comes to *how* you perform a particular job. If that same internal medicine doctor is really good at what he does, then he will be able to ask for higher fees, will have more referrals, will have a larger patient base, perhaps will be able to work in a more prestigious clinic or hospital, and so on. The subjective part of his value has to do with how he utilizes his strengths within the job.

When it comes to increasing your own income, you must discover both objective and subjective ways you can add more value. To do this, start with your strengths.

### Step 1: The Personal Value Enhancer

1. Take the list of strengths you developed in the exercise on page 127, and write each of them on the Personal Value Enhancer form.

2. Brainstorm all the ways you could use each strength to add more value at your present job. If you have a talent for graphic design, could you create a company newsletter or new marketing piece? If you're a salesperson who's really good at presentations, could you coach others or develop a new script for sales calls? Come up with as many ways as you can to add more value in your present position, job, or company.

3. Write down all the ways you could use this strength to add more value outside of your current job. If you're a great presenter, could you develop a sales training course? If you're great at systems, could you be a professional organizer? For almost anything you do well, there will be someone who will pay you to either teach them or do it for them. Brainstorm all the ways you could add more value outside of your current business and make more money in the process.

Many of the people who come to me for financial planning love their current jobs but don't see how they can add to their income. "I'm a teacher," or "I'm a social worker," they tell me. "I really love what I

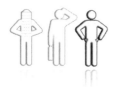

# Personal Value
# Enhancer™

$25K – 40hrs

$50K – ___hrs

$100K – ___hrs

| List 5 Things That You Can Do to Become More Valuable |
|---|
| 1 |
| 2 |
| 3 |
| 4 |
| 5 |

do, but there's no way I can make more money even if I add more value in my current job." But there's always a way to discover new avenues of income. You just have to be willing to find value in new and unexpected places.

Say I love carpentry, and a friend and I decide to go into business building custom-made desks and cabinets. I cut the wood and my friend glues the pieces together. One day my wife, Angie, decides to help out by sweeping up all the wood chips, sawdust, and scrap wood. Then she says, "If we added water and glue to the wood shavings and sawdust, we could make particleboard." One of the biggest furniture makers in the world, IKEA, created an entire business around affordable particleboard furniture. They found value in what others would consider waste.

Not too long ago a client of mine, a professor, told me that he was leaving the university to take a job as a consultant. "I train teachers and I love it, but I don't make enough to take care of my family the way I want to," he told me.

"Maybe there's a way you can use your strengths to create more income," I said. "Is there something you teach that no one else does that you could turn into a book?"

"Yes," he answered immediately. "And I have graduate students who can help with the research." Today, five years later, he makes a sizeable amount in royalties from the textbook and training program he developed. He still does what he loves—teaching teachers—because he was creative in adding value.

What can you do to increase your income by doing what you already do well and enjoy? Almost anything can be turned into an opportunity for making money. Hobbies, skills, strengths, and work experience all can form the basis of a new income stream. What's your "particleboard"—the value that can be created from the "wood shavings" of your talents? Are you a great cook who could sell your recipes online? A computer geek who can set up wireless networks in people's homes? A long-distance runner who could coach other runners? A math teacher who could offer classes to high school kids in money management? What products could you create from your expertise, experience, or strengths? Nowadays information-based products are easy to create. How many different ways can you come up with to increase your income?

## Step 2: The Income Opportunity Filter

When faced with multiple opportunities, some people become paralyzed. The Income Opportunity Filter will ensure that the opportunities you pursue will be most likely to give you the income you desire and fit into your vision, values, strengths, and goals.

1. Write at the top of a page the amount you wish to add to your current yearly income. Be realistic: if you're currently making $40,000 and you want to add $1 million, that's quite a jump in one year. However, doubling your income to $80,000 might be achievable if you increase what you earn at work and add another opportunity outside of your current job.

2. Make a list of your top three new opportunities from the list you brainstormed in the exercise on page 135. Using the following four criteria, you will evaluate each opportunity and rate it as a −1 (taking away value), +1 (adding value), or 0 (no effect either way).

a. *Vision:* How does this opportunity contribute to or detract from the vision of You, Inc.?

b. *Values:* Is this opportunity consistent with the values you described in your life blueprint? If family is your top value and this opportunity would require you to work weekends, you would rank it a −1. If it would allow you to work from home, it might be a +1.

c. *Financial Reward:* How much of a contribution will this make toward the financial goal you wrote down? Will the initial outlay be so high that this opportunity won't recoup its costs for several years? Will the financial reward justify the effort you must put into the opportunity?

d. *Strengths:* Does this opportunity utilize your strengths? Will it be something you will enjoy doing? Sometimes we can have expertise in something but not enjoy it enough to pursue an opportunity. You may love art but hate the idea of teaching art to children. However, you may love the idea of designing and marketing your own line of greeting cards.

3. Add up the total score for each opportunity and decide the minimum acceptable score for you to pursue it. Does it have to have +1s in every area, or in a majority of areas? Write down your conclusions about each opportunity. Is this something you wish to take action on immediately? Do you need more information? Do you need a partner to help you? Is it better to table this opportunity until another time? If none of these opportunities meets your criteria, what would have to change for them to become something you would pursue? Do you need to brainstorm other opportunities that would better suit your needs? Your goal is to create at least one additional income opportunity you can pursue this year.

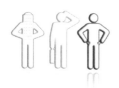

# The Income Opportunity Filter™

## Opportunity Filter

| Opportunity | Vision | Values | $ Reward | Strengths | Total | Minimum Acceptable Score |
|---|---|---|---|---|---|---|
| **A** | | | | | | |
| **B** | | | | | | |
| **C** | | | | | | |
| Scoring Scale | +1 | 0 | -1 | | | |

$$$ _____

## Conclusions

**A**

**B**

**C**

### Opportunity Decision

- ☐ Yes
- ☐ No

- ☐ Yes
- ☐ No

- ☐ Yes
- ☐ No

## Immediate Actions That Need to Be Taken

| 1 | 3 |
|---|---|
| 2 | 4 |

**4.** For the opportunity you have chosen, list four actions you can take to get started immediately. You could apply for a business license. You could create an ad for your local paper. You could find a partner. You could write a business blueprint. (I strongly suggest that the blueprint be the first action you take. See my book *Small Business, Big Life* or go to my Web site.) You could consult a professional for guidance. You could go out and buy supplies. You could test your market with an online ad.

Remember, you are choosing your income opportunities based on your strengths—things you are good at doing and enjoy. Therefore, doing more of these things should add to your life, not detract from it. They also should help you build on what you already do well rather than take you in a completely different direction. I see far too many people who try to make more income by choosing whatever is convenient, whether it draws upon their skills or not. This is the trap of multilevel marketing. People love the idea of a home-based business they can do "on the side," but fail to evaluate whether they have the strengths the business will require—communication and sales skills, the ability to self-motivate, financial abilities, and so on. You must use your strengths as the filter for choosing any opportunity. When you do, you are more likely to succeed in creating the income you desire while enjoying the work that you do.

Finally, it's better to choose one opportunity and succeed while having a life than try to get two businesses started and leave the rest of your life behind. The idea is not for you to create a situation where you feel even more overworked and overwhelmed just so you can increase your income. Remember, there are other ways to eliminate feeling underpaid. You can add more value at your current job and get paid more for it. You can cut your expenses and live within your means. You can change the conditions of your current work by reducing or eliminating unpaid overtime, getting more help with your job, or finding ways to use more of your strengths and less of your weaknesses. All of these will help you leave behind feelings of being underpaid, and step more fully into a life where you feel that you are well paid and successful because of the value you have given and received.

# CHAPTER FIVE

# From Stress to Success:
# The Gift of Giving Back

Imagine leaving your workplace at the end of the day. You've been busy, but you've dedicated your efforts to the projects and tasks that will make the greatest difference and utilize your talents to their highest degree. You've worked with others who are using talents that complement yours, and as a team, you've done more than any of you could accomplish alone. Your work has stretched you but not stressed you. You feel that you've contributed to a bigger purpose, whether it's the completion of a project; the support of your team; your personal success; and/or the success of your family, company, organization, or community. You feel that you are appreciated and well compensated, and you can look forward to greater compensation based upon the value you provide.

You also are able to leave your work at the workplace, instead of bringing it home with you. You spend time on family, relationships, and activities you enjoy, knowing that they make you feel at least as rich, if not more so, than the money you earn from your job. Work is a part of who you are, not your whole life. You live according to your values, focusing on the important areas of your life, fulfilling your roles, and nurturing the relationships in your life blueprint. Like everyone, you have to juggle the time and energy you devote to different parts of your life, but overall you're happy with what you accomplish. Your days of feeling habitually overworked, overwhelmed, and underpaid are reduced, if not completely gone. Instead of being stressed, you feel hope and possibility. You look for solutions rather than being caught up in problems. You are on the road from stress to success.

A definition of success tied to a certain income or a certain position or a certain lifestyle is often a recipe for feeling overworked, overwhelmed, and underpaid. On the other hand, if your definition of success is a life that is lived well and shared with others, you are more likely to enjoy the journey of your life instead of being stressed by it. I believe that success is *a life filled with enough money, time, love, and health to enjoy and share with others.* Success means being wealthy in everything that matters: inner resources like love, courage, compassion, determination, and integrity; riches of time for pursuits you enjoy; a healthy body and mind; fulfilling relationships with colleagues and friends; a supportive home environment; a spiritual connection with something greater than yourself; making a difference not just in the people you love but also in the lives of those less fortunate.

Two solutions that will inevitably lead you to greater success are *purpose* and *possibilities.* When you are living a life of purpose—one where you know who you are and why you are here—it's easier to keep your focus on what's truly important rather than allow yourself to get caught up in the "stuff" of daily life. It's also easier to see the possibilities that surround you at every moment. Feelings of being overworked, overwhelmed, and underpaid can blind you to the other options available in almost every circumstance. You think that you are trapped, and you are—simply because your vision has been blocked by your emotions. But when you can step out of those feelings, using the solutions, systems, and steps you learned in this book, you'll find a world of possibilities available to you that you never saw or thought possible to try.

Creating success through purpose and possibilities comes from five elements. First, everything you do must be put in the context of your *life purpose*, the reason you were born and the guide for your lifetime accomplishments. Second, your efforts must be underpinned by a strong *personal foundation* that will support you in the toughest times. Third, you must *evaluate your life* regularly, and step outside of your comfort zone so you will continue to grow and expand. Fourth, you must incorporate *gratitude and giving back* into your life. Finally, you must create *a lifetime legacy* of meaning for yourself and others. With these five elements, you'll find you can handle the inevitable challenges that life will bring, and experience the success and fulfillment you desire.

## Declaring Your Purpose in Life

Who are you? Why are you here? What were you born to do? It's all too easy to lose track of the big questions in the busyness of daily life. But if you don't know your purpose, your efforts are nothing *but* busyness, and you will lose the opportunity to make your life mean something. Declaring a purpose gives you a destination that will make each step of the journey of life more significant and intentional. It also will help you get back on track should you get lost in the urgent yet inconsequential demands of life.

Your purpose can be very intimate or very large. It can be to be a great parent, or the best woodworker the world has ever known, or to inspire millions with your example. Your purpose can be to provide a happy life for your family, or to mentor others to be their best. Your true purpose has three elements. First, it must *excite you.* It should energize you in the morning, and you should feel great having accomplished it when you go to bed at night. Second, it must *feel true to your innermost being.* Some people try to create a "politically correct" version of their purpose—"I want to save the world"—or live a purpose that a parent or mentor wants for them rather than one that's really theirs. Your purpose must represent whatever is true for you in your heart of hearts. Third, it must be *something you can work on for most of your life.* Being a great parent is a purpose that will last for as long as you have children. Being the best at your chosen profession could be part of your greater purpose of developing your abilities and skills to their utmost and using them to benefit the world. A life purpose should guide the journey of your life and you should measure your efforts by it.

You already may have an idea of your purpose. You can use the following process and the Personal Purpose Triad form to capture your thoughts.

1. Sit quietly and reflect upon your life so far. What are the main themes of your life? What have you focused on? What were you doing when you felt the most fulfilled and "on purpose"? What

events would you consider the highlights of your life to date? Jot down your answers.

2. Looking at your notes, which aspects stand out as the most important? Being the best? Making a difference? Learning and growing? Helping others? Creating a great family? Mentoring people? Figuring things out and creating systems? Pushing past your limits? Write down anything that might be part of your purpose.

3. Now, ask yourself, "If someone asked me, 'What's the purpose of your life?' what would I say?" Start writing whatever comes up. It can be simple and short, or long and elaborate. Don't censor yourself—just write until you're done.

4. Try and distill your purpose into one or two sentences. Imagine you are creating an epitaph to be carved on your tombstone. If it reflected your purpose in life, what would it say? Write your purpose in the middle of the Personal Purpose Triad.

5. Next to the sides of the Personal Purpose Triad you'll see three lines for the qualities or emotions that will help you fulfill your purpose. What three words describe who you are and what you want to do? Which qualities or emotions do you need to embody? If your purpose is to be the best, would determination and courage help you? If you want to be a great parent, will you need love and patience? If you want to inspire others, how about vision, passion, or clarity? My three words are *instruct, inspire,* and *impact.* They sum up my purpose and remind me of how I will achieve it. Come up with your own list of qualities or emotions that will help you fulfill your purpose, and write them below the Triad. Then choose the three most important ones and write them next to the Triad's sides.

When you feel overworked, overwhelmed, or underpaid, it's usually because you are (1) too focused on your career, or (2) being pulled in different directions by the demands of your life. Both of these problems usually arise when you are unclear about your ultimate purpose. On the other hand, when you know why you are here, when you declare to yourself and the world that you have a purpose and take action to make that purpose real, then you are more likely to put your focus on what will give you the greatest fulfillment over the long term. Human beings will do more and create greater results when they know why they are working. Dedicated soldiers tell you, "We know what we are fighting for." Mothers say, "I know that what I do will help my children." Doctors say, "My life is dedicated to helping my patients." Purpose can help you, too, create a drive and direction for your life by clarifying what's important. It will point you toward the tasks, choices, and options that will make the biggest difference. Ultimately, your purpose will help you look back over your life and feel that what you accomplished was worth the effort.

## Your Personal Foundation

If you've felt overworked, overwhelmed, and underpaid, you know how easy it is to get into the habits that create those feelings, and how hard it can be to pull yourself out. Knowing and living the purpose of your life will help you move forward and give you greater focus, but it's all too easy to let circumstances distract you and take over your days. To experience the kind of success and drive you need to fulfill your purpose, you must develop a strong personal foundation.

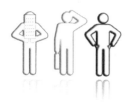

# Personal Purpose Triad™

List 3 Words That Describe the Essence of
Who You Are or Who You Want to Be

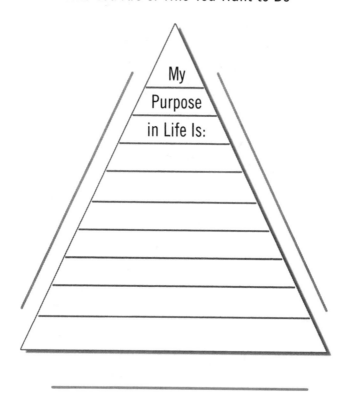

My
Purpose
in Life Is:

Every building has some kind of foundation. Your house's foundation only goes down a few feet, but the foundation of a skyscraper must be stronger and deeper to support the weight of the building above it. In the same way, to build the kind of life that will give you the greatest success and fulfillment, you must make sure that the foundation underlying your life is deep and strong.

A personal foundation includes your *character*, your *standards* for yourself and others, your *morals*, and your *ethics*. Year by year you have created this personal foundation by what you learned from your family and your environment, and by the choices you made at home, at work, with yourself, and with others. Few of us can clearly describe the elements of our personal foundation, yet our character, standards, morals, and ethics influence everything we do. Ultimately, they will determine *how* we achieve success. A personal foundation will either hold us up in the tough times or crumble beneath our feet.

Every day you're either strengthening your foundation or weakening it by the choices you make and the actions you take. Living by your word strengthens your foundation; not keeping commitments weakens it. Setting standards and living by them even when it's uncomfortable strengthen your foundation; letting things slide weakens it. Delivering value on the job or to your family strengthens your foundation; doing just enough to get by weakens it. While strengthening your personal foundation isn't rocket science, it's rarely easy. Yet having a strong personal foundation ultimately makes life far less complicated, because you will have a clear set of principles to guide your choices.

Use the following exercise to describe your personal foundation:

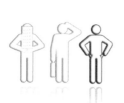

# Personal Foundation Excavator™

| Your Character | Your Standards | Your Morals | Your Ethics |
|---|---|---|---|
| 1 | | | |
| 2 | | | |
| 3 | | | |
| 4 | | | |
| 5 | | | |

| List 5 Things You Do That Weaken Your Foundation | List 5 Things You Do (or can do) To Strengthen Your Foundation |
|---|---|
| 1 | 1 |
| 2 | 2 |
| 3 | 3 |
| 4 | 4 |
| 5 | 5 |

1. List the most important aspects of (a) your character, (b) your standards, (c) your morals, and (d) your ethics. Under "Character," for example, you might write, "I am honest," "I value others," "I am a good friend," or "I go the extra mile." Under "Standards," you might put, "I do my best," "I work hard," "I set clear boundaries for myself," or "I expect others to be honest with me." Under "Morals," you would write things like, "I believe in forgiveness," "I would never lie," and "Do unto others as you would have them do unto you." For "Ethics," you might include, "I respect others' rights," "I would never steal," and "I charge fair value for the effort I provide." Write both what you will do and what you would never do.

2. List at least five things you do that weaken your foundation. Do you procrastinate? Use social lies to get out of uncomfortable situations? Hold a grudge? Put others down? Cheat at work or in your relationships? It's better to get these things out in the open than let them continue to undermine your foundation. How can you avoid doing these things in the future?

3. List at least five things you do (or can do) to strengthen your foundation. Can you speak more kindly to a co-worker? Be truthful with your friend or spouse about your feelings? Stop cutting corners at work? Apologize or forgive? Make a commitment to yourself to do at least one of these things within a week, and continue to look for ways to strengthen your foundation.

A strong personal foundation makes it easier for you to take on greater responsibilities and greater opportunities, because you know your own personal ground rules in any circumstance. A good foundation provides the immovable and solid support on which to build even greater levels of success.

## Your Life Evaluation

Have you ever climbed a tall hill or a mountain? You walk upward for a very long time, and it can seem that you're making no progress. Then you reach a vista point, look down, and are amazed at how far you've climbed. Life's like that: you work on something for a long time and don't see much progress until you take a moment to assess how far you've come. To truly feel the successes you are creating in your life, you need to evaluate your progress regularly.

Your life evaluation is composed of three parts. First, every three to six months you need to *check how you feel*. Are you more fulfilled or less? Happier or the same? More stressed or less? What's working well for you? Where are you still having challenges? How do you feel about your success with the values, life focus areas, roles, and relationships you described in your life blueprint? What would you need to focus on more to be even happier?

Now let's get specific. On a scale of 1 to 10, 1 being none and 10 being completely, how much are you currently feeling overworked, overwhelmed, and underpaid? What's changed for the better? What's still the same? What, if anything, is worse? What actions do you need to take to handle any remaining negative feelings? Remember, feeling overworked, overwhelmed, and underpaid was a process of accumulated stresses and challenges. Leaving those feelings behind also will be a process, of responding differently to the same challenges and creating new possibilities from your new resources and reactions. Don't beat yourself up if you aren't out of the woods yet; just change what you're doing. Go back and review the exercises in this book and recommit to taking the actions that will help you reduce or eliminate these feelings from your life.

Second, you must *check your progress on your life purpose.* What have you done to live your purpose more fully? Spend a few moments to acknowledge even your smallest accomplishments. Human beings are good at beating themselves up for what they haven't achieved and terrible at celebrating their wins. Make a list of at least ten ways you are fulfilling your life purpose, and a second list of five things you are committed to doing to live your purpose even more fully in the next three months. At your next life evaluation, you'll check your progress on these five items, celebrate your wins, and recommit to these items and/or add new ones to your list.

Third, you must *stretch yourself and step out of your comfort zone.* Most people become overworked, overwhelmed, and underpaid when they feel the demands placed upon them are greater than they can stand. You've learned many ways to handle the situations that created those demands, but there's another way to cope: by expanding your comfort zone. When the challenges become bigger, *you* must become bigger. You must become comfortable with the higher level of demand placed upon you.

It's like going to the gym. If you keep exercising with the same five-pound weights, you'll achieve a certain level of fitness but you won't grow beyond that level. To increase your muscles, you must stress them beyond what's comfortable. You must add weight to your workout. As you look at your own life, you must identify the areas where you are firmly stuck in your comfort zone and need some additional "weight

# Life Evaluation™

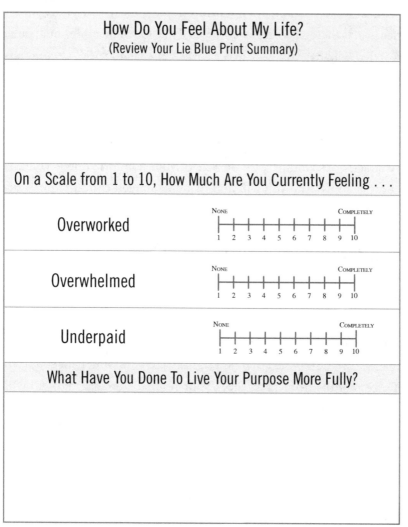

## How Do You Feel About My Life?
### (Review Your Lie Blue Print Summary)

### On a Scale from 1 to 10, How Much Are You Currently Feeling . . .

**Overworked**

NONE                    COMPLETELY
1  2  3  4  5  6  7  8  9  10

**Overwhelmed**

NONE                    COMPLETELY
1  2  3  4  5  6  7  8  9  10

**Underpaid**

NONE                    COMPLETELY
1  2  3  4  5  6  7  8  9  10

### What Have You Done To Live Your Purpose More Fully?

training" to increase your results. This might not feel good, especially in the beginning, but eventually you'll be able to handle the increased weight with ease.

Stepping out of your comfort zone can take many forms. One of the best ways is to seek out opportunities that make you a little apprehensive. Is there a project at work you'd like to volunteer for but you're worried whether you can carry it off? A chance to speak at your volunteer group or to lead a team, and you've never done either? Someone you'd like to ask on a date but you're afraid of being rejected? A physical challenge—like a marathon, a ski weekend, whitewater rafting, or skydiving—that scares and excites you at the same time? Taking on such activities will increase the size of your comfort zone beyond its current limits. And you will find that an enlarged comfort zone usually means an enlarged and happier life as well.

Choose at least one action you will take in the next three months to step out of your comfort zone. Whatever action you choose should create at least a little fear for you, a sense that it's beyond your current capabilities. If possible, it also should excite you when you think about the results. Do something within the next two days to start the ball rolling. (When stepping out of your comfort zone, it's best to treat it like an injection—the faster you start, the less fear and pain you feel.) Three months from now, check your results. How have you grown? Who have you become? What new ways of thinking, believing, and acting have you developed? How have your internal "muscles" increased? How much more can you handle in your life because you have stretched outside your comfort zone? Like standing at the top of a hill looking down to where you started climbing, you may be amazed at how much you have grown.

# Life Evaluation™

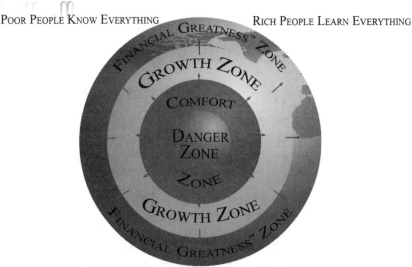

| Choose At Least One Action You Will Take in the Next Three Months to Step Out of Your Comfort Zone |
|---|
|  |
| How Have You Grown? |
|  |

## The Real Secret: Gratitude and Giving to Others

When you feel overworked, overwhelmed, and underpaid, you are coming from lack. You don't have enough time; you don't have the resources to handle everything you have to do; you aren't getting paid enough. You're focusing on what you don't have enough of rather than appreciating how much you already enjoy. That's the real secret to success, and ultimately the secret to banish feelings of being overworked, overwhelmed, and underpaid from your life forever. You must *be grateful for what you have, and give of what you have to others.*

Have you ever been stressed and focusing on a problem, and your child comes in and gives you a hug? If you take a moment to appreciate their gesture, how much better do you feel? If you're overwhelmed with all the e-mail in your inbox, and then you read an encouraging message from a dear friend, how much less do the other messages bother you? If you're worrying about money, and your spouse arranges to have your neighbor babysit the kids so you can spend an evening together at home, how much value do you place on the date that costs nothing but means so much? Sometimes we can't change our circumstances, but we *always* can change how we feel simply by finding something for which to be grateful. Gratitude crowds out fear. It also crowds out the sense of lack that underlies feeling overworked, overwhelmed, or underpaid. Whenever I start feeling pressured or sorry for myself, I think, *Man, I've got a good income, a great career, a wonderful spouse and great kids. I'm lucky and blessed. I've got a lot to be grateful for.* Gratitude and appreciation are the truest manifestations of success and fulfillment.

I suggest that all my clients keep a gratitude journal. Either daily, weekly, or at least monthly, they write down seven things for which they are grateful. Each time they review the list, they ask themselves, "Why am I grateful for this? What has this brought into my life? What gift has this been for me?" I also suggest that they say a prayer or offer some kind of thanks to God for these gifts. Actively feeling gratitude daily will enrich your life more than any other practice. It will help you appreciate what you have and open you to receive even more.

Most people would agree that when they feel gratitude, they feel more abundant, and the natural next step is to give back to others. But I believe that the cycle works the other way as well. When we give to others, we feel more abundant, and we experience more gratitude. Have you ever had only a few dollars in your pocket, but you dropped one of those dollars in the collection plate at church, or placed it in the Salvation Army kettle, or gave it to a homeless person? I'll bet that the value you received from giving that dollar away far outstripped its buying power. Giving to others is part of a prosperity mind-set. It tells the subconscious mind, if not the entire universe, that you have more than enough for your own needs and can share your wealth with others. This kind of giving extends beyond financial means. You can share your time and talents as well as treasure. When you give your time to help others, you signal that you have enough time for what's important. When you give of your efforts, you signal that you have enough value to share. When you give of your love and caring, you signal that you have an abundance of love in your life. Remember, the definition of success is having more than enough time, value, love, energy, and wealth to share. If you ever feel overworked, overwhelmed, or underpaid again, find something to be grateful for and some way you can give to others, and you'll immediately feel more successful and happier too.

# Your Lifetime Legacy

Remember in chapter 1 you visualized being at your own funeral and saw two different versions of how your life was viewed by others. But the truth is, you are creating that legacy every minute of your life. It's up to you to choose how you will live and what you will be remembered for. Just like your life purpose, writing your lifetime legacy is a powerful tool that will help guide your choices. Take a few minutes to do the following:

1. Close your eyes and imagine your funeral. Who is there? What are they saying about you? Were you loved by many people? Were you recognized as a leader in your business or community? What are the aspects of your life that people talk about the most?

2. See the person who stands up to deliver your eulogy. What do they say about you? Are you happy with what they have to say? What would have the most meaning if it were included in your eulogy?

3. Open your eyes and write the legacy you wish to leave behind when you die. What effect have you had on the world? What have you accomplished? What relationships have been important? What contributions have you made? What did you do with your time on earth? What were you grateful for? What was your legacy? Think of this as a combination of a last testament and obituary. State what you want to have said about you by those you know and the world as a whole.

Ultimately, true success has little to do with the results of your life and everything to do with how you feel about what you have done

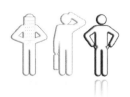 # Lifetime Legacy Lamp™

## What Kind of Legacy Would You Like to Leave Behind?

with your days on earth. We're all heading for the same destination, which is six feet under. On most grave markers, you'll see the person's name and their birth and death dates with a dash in between. Ultimately, what is truly important is not the date of your death or birth, but how you live during that dash. And it *is* a dash: your life will be over before you know it. Your job will be done and your children grown; you will have made your contribution to the world—or not—in the blink of an eye. How you live the dash will determine how happy you are and the quality of the legacy you leave behind.

## A Life of Fulfillment

As authors of great books have told us for hundreds of years, success is not about what we achieve as much as how we achieve it. If your prior efforts to achieve success left you overworked, overwhelmed, and underpaid, then I hope you have learned to change your ways. Success has more to do with who you become in the process of its achievement. You will know you are successful when you feel profound peace of mind, happiness, joy, abundance, and confidence; when you are living the life you designed, one in which you are pursuing dreams that have meaning for you and those you love; and when you feel grateful for the life you have been given, and eager to share your gifts of time, talent, and treasure with others.

Will there be challenges? Always. As Norman Vincent Peale said, the only people with no problems are in the cemetery. "Problems are a sign of life," he said. Problems are also a signal that it's time for you to expand your comfort zone so you can handle greater responsibilities and greater opportunities. It may not be easy, but it always will be worth putting in the effort to expand and grow past your current limits.

Real success is a treasure you cannot spend or lose, and it can't ever be stolen from you, because it is who you have become. When you are living a life in which you are following your dreams, and those dreams make life better not only for you but also for those you love, your community, and perhaps even the world as a whole, then your success is assured. People will be filled with love and appreciation for your life. And you can feel pride and great peace of mind, knowing the world is better for your having spent time on it.

I wish you an exciting and fulfilling journey from stress to success!

# Resources

For all the forms utilized in this book as well as two bonus chapters, please go to: www.louisbarajas.com.

# References

**Books:**

Bach, David. *The Automatic Millionaire: A Powerful One-Step Plan to Live and Finish Rich.* New York: Broadway Books, 2003.

Barajas, Louis. *The Latino Journey to Financial Greatness: The 10 Steps to Creating Wealth, Security, and a Prosperous Future for You and Your Family.* New York: HarperCollins, 2003.

——————. *Small Business, Big Life: Five Steps to Creating a Great Life with Your Own Small Business.* Nashville, TN: Thomas Nelson, Inc., 2007.

Collins, Jim. *Good to Great: Why Some Companies Make the Leap . . . and Others Don't.* New York: HarperCollins, 2001.

Eker, T. Harv. *Secrets of the Millionaire Mind: Mastering the Inner Game of Wealth.* New York: HarperBusiness, 2005.

Ferriss, Timothy. *The 4-Hour Workweek: Escape 9–5, Live Anywhere, and Join the New Rich.* New York: Crown Publishers, 2007.

Rath, Tom. *StrengthsFinder 2.0.* New York: Gallup Press, 2007.

Sullivan, Dan. *The Laws of Lifetime Growth: Always Make Your Future*

*Bigger than Your Past*. San Francisco: Berrett-Koehler Publishers, 2006.

Ury, William. *The Power of a Positive No: Save the Deal, Save the Relationship—and Still Say No*. New York: Bantam Books, 2007.

## Reports and Articles:

Bernstein, Jared, and Lawrence Mishel. "Economy's Gains Fail to Reach Most Workers' Paychecks." EPI Briefing Paper #195, Economic Policy Institute, Washington, D.C., September 3, 2007.

Bond, James T., with Cindy Thompson, Ellen Galinsky, and David Prottas. "Highlights of the 2002 National Study of the Changing Workforce: Executive Summary." New York: Families and Work Institute, 2002.

Galinsky, Ellen. "Dual-Centric: A New Concept of Work-Life." Condensed from *Leaders in a Global Economy* by Ellen Galinsky, Kimberlee Salmond, and James T. Bond of Families and Work Institute; Marcia Brumit Kropf and Meredith Moore of Catalyst; and Brad Harrington of Boston Center for Work & Family. New York: Families and Work Institute, 2003.

————, James T. Bond, Stacy S. Kim, Lois Backon, Erin Brownfield, and Kelly Sakai. "Overwork in America: When the Way We Work Becomes Too Much: Executive Summary." New York: Families and Work Institute, 2004.

————, Stacy S. Kim, and James T. Bond. *Feeling Overworked: When Work Becomes Too Much*. New York: Families and Work Institute, 2001.

Hout, Michael, and Caroline Hanley. *The Overworked American Family: Trends and Nontrends in Working Hours, 1968-2001*. "A Century of

Difference" Working Paper. Berkeley: The Survey Research Center, University of California, Berkeley, 2002.

Mishel, Lawrence, Jared Bernstein, and Sylvia Allegretto. "The State of Working America 2006/2007." A report issued by the Economic Policy Institute. Ithaca, NY: Cornell University Press, 2007.

"Questions and Answers about Generation X/Generation Y: A Sloan Work & Family Research Network Fact Sheet." Sloan Work and Family Research Network, Boston College Graduate School of Social Work. Chestnut Hill, MA: December 2006.

"Questions and Answers about Overwork: A Sloan Work & Family Research Network Fact Sheet." Sloan Work and Family Research Network, Boston College Graduate School of Social Work. Chestnut Hill, MA: December 2006.

Reh, F. John, "Pareto's Principle: The 80-20 Rule," published online at www.management.about.com/cs/generalmanagement/a/Pareto 081202.htm.

"Salary.com Survey Reveals Disconnect Between Employers' Perceptions on Employee Job Satisfaction Factors and Why Employees Stay or Leave a Job." Press release dated January 30, 2006. www. salary.com, Waltham, MA.

Senior, Jennifer. "Can't Get No Satisfaction." *New York Magazine,* November 27, 2006.

"25-Year Trend Data Facts." Families and Work Institute Paper, New York, 2002.

Webster, Bruce H., Jr., and Alemayehu Bishaw, U.S. Census Bureau, American Community Survey Reports, ACS-08, *Income, Earnings, and Poverty Data from the 2006 American Community Survey,* U.S. Government Printing Office, Washington, D.C., 2007.

"Work, Stress, and Health," National Institute for Occupational Safety & Health Conference, 1999.

**Web Sites:**

www.bc.edu/cwf (The Boston College for Work & Family)
www.carddata.com
www.cardtrak.com
www.epi.org (The Economic Policy Institute)
www.familiesandwork.org (Families and Work Institute)
www.4hourworkweek.com
www.salary.com

Overworked, Overwhelmed, and Underpaid

# Acknowledgments

No man or woman can ever achieve any level of success without the help of a life mate. Angie is my better half, and I mean that with all sincerity. She makes me a much more loving person than I could ever be on my own.

Aaron Muñoz and Gilbert Cerda, my partners at Louis Barajas, Wealth Planning, give me wings to fly. They take all my material and tools and use them to change the lives of our clients on a daily basis. My staff, Isabel and Diane, keep our firm running seamlessly. My stepson, Eddie Romero, has been a great help in creating all the many forms our clients use to plan their lives and financial future.

Victoria St. George of Just Write Literary & Editorial Partners, LLC, has been my writing partner from the beginning. She takes my words and gives them the extra touch that allows me to express myself in ways that are special.

The team at Thomas Nelson has tremendous faith in my work. Thank you for your commitment to my message and helping me get it to the ends of the earth.

To Shannon Miser-Marven, my literary agent of Dupree Miller & Associates: thanks for not giving up on me. As a small fish in your big pond, you still manage to take the time to take care of me.

To my previous and current sponsors: I can't thank you enough. In the past you have opened up the doors to opportunities that have sustained my writing career. You help share my message by giving others access to my books when they might never have read them otherwise.

To all my clients and readers who believe that financial planning is about a human experience, not just a money experience: thank you for your confidence and faith in our results.

Finally, thank you to my parents and my in-laws, who provide Angie and me with endless emotional support and unconditional love. Whenever Angie and I fall into the trap of feeling overworked, overwhelmed, and underpaid, you show us what it means to be truly successful and abundant no matter how much money someone has in the bank. Because of you, we are better people. Because of your support, our lives are a lot less stressed and a lot happier.

# About the Author

Louis Barajas is the financial and business advisor to people who are making a difference in their own fields of endeavor. He has created a firm for clients who are inspired to create wealth and use their money to live a better life. His clients are influential people who want to work with someone they can trust to manage their investments and help them make important financial decisions. Other clients are people who have more desire than money, but are committed to creating the kind of wealth that will help them reach their full potential.

Louis is a nationally recognized expert in financial and business issues. In his books, speeches, workshops, and consulting, Louis makes the complex and overwhelming world of finance and small business comprehensible, as he teaches people the powerful and practical strategies to achieve Financial Greatness™.